What Is Sexual Capital?

These are just snapshots of a postindustrial, global and mediatic regime that [. . .] I will call *pharmapornographic*. *The term refers to the processes of a biomolecular (pharmaco) and semiotic-technical (pornographic) government of sexual subjectivity.* [. . .] There is nothing to discover in sex or in sexual identity; there is no *inside*. The truth about sex is not a disclosure. It is *sexdesign*. Pharmacopornographic biocapitalism does not produce *things*. It produces mobile ideas, living organs, symbols, desires, chemical reactions and conditions of the soul. In biotechnology and in pornocommunication there is no object to be produced. The pharmacopornographic business is the *invention of a subject* and then its global reproduction.

Paul B. Preciado, *Testo Junkie*,
New York 2013, 33–6

What Is Sexual Capital?

Dana Kaplan
Eva Illouz

polity

This English edition first published in 2022 by Polity Press

Polity Press
65 Bridge Street
Cambridge CB2 1UR, UK

Polity Press
101 Station Landing
Suite 300
Medford, MA 02155, USA

ISBN-13: 978-1-5095-5231-3
ISBN-13: 978-1-5095-5232-0 (pb)

A catalogue record for this book is available from the British Library.

Library of Congress Control Number: 2021946299

Typeset in 12.50n 15pt Adobe Garamond
by Cheshire Typesetting Ltd, Cuddington, Cheshire
Printed and bound in Great Britain by TJ Books Ltd, Padstow, Cornwall

For further information on Polity, visit our website:
politybooks.com

Contents

Acknowledgments

Dana Kaplan's research for this book was supported by the ISRAEL SCIENCE FOUNDATION (grant No. 1560/18) and by the Open University of Israel's Research Authority. She wishes to thank Roy Zunder and Rona Mashiach for their invaluable assistance.

Ella and Gal, this is for you.

Introduction

Sex and Sociological Metaphors

Two sociologists have recently called on their pro-
fession to be more modest, more ambitious and
more joyful in its endeavor to explain the social
world.[1] While sociology cannot make the world a
better place, they go on to claim, it can certainly
offer fresh ways of understanding it through its
theories, concepts, and metaphors. In this study
we scrutinize one sociological metaphor that has
been gaining considerable traction: that of sexual
capital, which is increasingly being used—and
not only by sociologists, gender scholars, and sex
researchers. In everyday talk sexual capital has
become a common metaphor for addressing the
actual social and individual consequences of "our
world made sexy" and how people "make do."[2]

Ordinary people will cringe at the use of capital for a domain like sexuality: after all, isn't sexuality a realm of pleasure, self-abandon, improvisation, play? Why should we connect it to the economic–sociological metaphor of capital? It is because sexuality is always "in society" and is regulated by changing societal forces. The three monotheistic religions have relentlessly regulated sexuality, making it central to the ideology of purity, to the family, and to political power. The way sexuality appears in ideals of the self is always social. If in the traditional world sexuality was shaped by religion, in late modernity it has become chiefly intertwined with the economy.

The metaphor of sexual capital assumes that sex is a resource for future gains in a way that goes well beyond sexual activity per se. Unlike concepts whose meanings, at least in theory, are widely shared and accepted, metaphors are more open and less precise. They have a certain vehicular quality, and it is their conceptual imprecision that sometimes makes them useful to the sociologist's imagination.[3] But, although the sexual capital metaphor has become quite popular, on the whole it remains undertheorized.

In common sociological usage, sexual capital refers to the returns people may receive from investing money, time, knowledge, and affective energy in constructing and enhancing their sexual self, the aspect of their identity that concerns sexuality. Some may opt for plastic surgery in a bid to beautify their face or body, while others may consume popular sex advice or join 'seduction communities' in order to train their sexual subjectivity to become more confident. These different investments may generate a better position from which to compete on sexual access to the bodies of others. This sexual competition can be oriented toward pleasure maximization or toward the mere feeling of being desired by others.

In this study we will describe the historical conditions under which four different forms of sexual capital have appeared, thrived, and sometimes waned. We will further suggest that under neoliberalism these forms of sexual capital change, and their transformation is responsible for phenomena as diverse as Silicone Valley sex parties as expressions of high-tech ideals of creative, fun, and collaborative work, genital plastic surgery among upper-middle-class patients, and even some sex workers' beliefs that through their services they are able to garner self-esteem and develop emotional resilience and other employable skills.[4] Through the lens of capital, we offer a detailed analysis of the effects of neoliberal capitalism on sex and sexuality. Neoliberal sexual capital, as we dub it, designates the ability to glean self-appreciation from sexual encounters and to use this self-value so as to foster employability.

To be sure, the idea that sexuality may increase one's self-value is not new. After all, the character of *Don Juan* offers a paradigm of masculinity in which sexual conquests are undertaken for their own sake, independently of marriage and institutions, because they presumably confer a value to the self. Don Juan embodies an attribute of masculinity increasingly independent of the power of the church and defined by a capacity to generate desire in women and to satisfy the subject's own desires. Such masculinity appears as a form of domination over women when a man like Don Juan would ruin their reputation and leave them without their only resource on the marriage market, namely their virginity. Yet, at least in Molière's play and in Mozart's opera, that character was punished by God himself, which thus suggests that, for serial sexuality to gener-

4

ate a socially recognized value to the self, it must be embedded in a social and normative order that makes it operative. In fact, in the era when Christianity was dominant, women were by default defined by a sort of sexual capital, namely by chastity. In traditional marriage markets, the woman's (and, to a lesser extent, the man's) reputation depended on virginity. Chastity—the lack of sexual activity—thus played the role of signaling woman's conformity to Christian ideals, thereby increasing her value. By default, sexuality played an important role in mate selection, because in traditional societies a marriage market was based both on reputation and on the economic assets of the prospective mate. In many ways, it is this normative order, which protected women from predators, that Don Juan challenges; and in consequence his sexuality is still highly constrained by the normative order of Christian patriarchy. For a full-fledged sexual capital to emerge, sexuality needs to autonomize itself vis-à-vis religion.[5] What has enabled the formation of a sexual capital is the loosening of the norms and taboos that regulate sexuality, along with the increasing incorporation of sexuality into the economic field. When sexuality

5

becomes structured by economic strategies, yields economic advantages, and becomes key to the economic sphere itself, we speak of sexual capital organized in a neoliberal culture, or neoliberal sexual capital.

Our understanding of neoliberal sexual capital in particular should be distinguished from three main arguments that are usually brought up when thinking about the relationship between sex and capitalism. These are: sex as redress to gender imbalances; sexual identities as a platform for sexual citizenship; and sexual commodification or the monetization of sexuality. Let us briefly address each of the three and explain how our approach to neoliberal sexual capital may differ, improve, or complement them.

First, we write against a well-known and controversial conceptualization of sexual capital by sociologist Catherine Hakim, who has defined erotic capital as a (markedly feminine) personal asset that women can use in the labor market and in intimate relations. In her view, erotic capital combines "beauty, sex appeal, liveliness, a talent for dressing well, charm and social skills and sexual competence. It is a mixture of physical and social attractiveness"—and these, she claims, can be capitalized on to get better jobs or negotiate "better deals" in intimate relationships.[6] Catherine Hakim's understanding of erotic capital points to a real and powerful social reality, made more acutely relevant by the various industries that use, exploit, and expose the (woman's) body: sexuality, as an attribute of the person, became increasingly transformed into an economic asset. However, hers remains a crude and limited way to define sexual capital, and for a number of reasons. For one thing, Hakim is oblivious to the historical and cultural processes that enabled the transformation of sexuality into capital. For example, media industries have been a major source for the codification of standards of beauty and for the conversion of beauty into capital in social fields. This process was driven by powerful economic interests. By treating sexual capital as if it were an obvious, unobtrusive attribute of "attractive" women, Hakim did not ask herself why attractiveness plays a role in various social fields that enable it to function as a capital. Second, Hakim made sexual capital an attribute of women, thereby accepting and reinforcing not only sex stereotypes but the very ways in which women are dominated, that is, through their bodies. Hakim in other words fails to understand that, if sexuality is a form of capital, this is because it uses attributes that also maintain the domination of women by men. As Catharine MacKinnon has cogently argued, sexuality is to heterosexual relationships what work is to the capitalist producer: the privileged site for the exploitation of women by men.[7] Even more surprising, perhaps, is that Hakim's understanding of sexual capital is premised on the hypothesis that there is a natural, biological male lust that women can use for their advancement: she seems oblivious to the fact that the use of women for sexual purposes and women's use of their own sexuality have always been part and parcel of the most oppressive form of patriarchy, not of its subversion. What characterizes patriarchy is *precisely* the fact that sexuality has represented an almost exclusive avenue for unwealthy and statusless women to gain status and social mobility—a fact that reflected their legal or economic disenfranchisement.

Instead of glibly viewing sexual capital as a way to empower women, we assume that sexual capital does not reverse the enduringly gendered nature of sexual scripts and the infamous sexual double standard (despite mounting evidence that young

8

women's sexuality has become more agentic and desiring). Nor does it transform the central role of gender and sexuality in organizing the division of household labor, the workplace dynamic, and the overall sex–gender structure of society.[8]

We also diverge from a second, very broad set of propositions that connect sexuality and capitalism through the notion of sexual citizenship and related scholarship that examines political and social struggles for the inclusion of sexual minorities.[9] In this short space we obviously cannot do justice to this very expansive field, which is informed by queer theory, political theory, and the sociology of neoliberalism. We shall therefore focus mainly on the relationship between claiming sexual rights and market participation.

Generally speaking, "sexual citizenship refers to the gendered, embodied, spatialized claims to sexual entitlements (including free expression, bodily autonomy, institutional inclusion) and sexual responsibilities (non-exploitation and non-oppression of others)."[10] Once sexual citizenship is defined this way, it becomes clear that issues related to it—for example sexual violence, sexual consent, or the rights of sex workers— are relevant to the entire population.[11] From the onset, however, the expansive body of work on citizenship and sexuality was primarily focused on claims for legal equality made by sexual minorities and continues to develop in this direction.[12] The field of sexual citizenship studies may be more theoretically diverse than before and includes a wider range of issues, which are addressed from various critical points of view (in what follows we elaborate on one of these critical accounts). Yet, although sexual citizenship studies have gone beyond the issue of the formal rights of sexual minorities,[13] LGBTQ+ emancipatory sexual politics still continues to be the focal point of this subdiscipline.[14]

In the next pages we briefly discuss one critical account of sexual citizenship.[15] The account suggests that the expansion of sexual rights and the mainstreaming of sexual diversity broadly go hand in hand with neoliberal capitalism. Our examination of this view will lay the grounds for the subsequent discussion of our own concept of neoliberal sexual capital, which, we argue, adds a missing layer to this otherwise important critical assessment of sexual citizenship.

What, then, is the connection between neoliberal capitalism and the expansion of sexual citizenship rights? According to the critical argument, reclaimed queer sexual identities may help legitimize, maintain, and reinforce neoliberal capitalism.[16] Such a view assumes that sexual democratization is simultaneously inclusionary of some people and exclusionary of others.[17] This, in turn, may determine who is seen as deserving various state provisions and protections and who isn't.[18] Thus delineated, the boundaries between deserving and undeserving sexual citizens also determine their differential relations to capital.[19]

One area in which sexual citizenship explicitly determines subjects' relations to capital is employment; the other is consumer culture. In the workplace, some "respectable" performances of homosexuality and queerness seem to have become acceptable. Yet transsexuals and gender-queer people still find it extremely difficult to enter middle-class professions and maintain their jobs.[20] Similarly, in the realm of consumption and lifestyle commodities, neoliberal capitalism not only "created a domesticated and consumerist gay identity"[21] but also increased "queer visibility in commodity culture," as Rosemary Hennessy puts it.[22] Public displays of queer activism, more positive representations of queer identities and lifeworlds in popular culture, and, finally, the lifestylization[23] of queer existence more broadly have all contributed to the commodification of queer identities, embodied styles, and other cultural codes and artifacts.

The relationship between consumer culture and differential sexual citizenship operates at the transnational level, too. Projects of sexual citizenship tend to fall into what Clare Hemmings calls "the lure of the modern," whereas sexual tolerance marks modern nations' levels of democracy and openness to global business.[24] Jasbir Puar famously coined the term "homonationalism" "for understanding the complexities of how 'acceptance' and 'tolerance' for gay and lesbian subjects have become a barometer by which the right to and capacity for national sovereignty is evaluated."[25] Moreover, tolerance for minority sexual identities on a national scale may exacerbate lucrative practices of pinkwashing such as gay tourism. Tel Aviv, a city considered a gay capital and located in a country that practices violent military occupation, is a case in point. [26]

To conclude, the critical premises of sexual citizenship that we have just outlined seem to suggest that a reformist and inclusionary sexual politics does nothing but fling about "progressive neoliberalism" buzzwords. Notions such as "sexual diversity" and "empowerment" only help mask capital's interests.[27] Nancy Fraser's contention that these sexual struggles have actually helped "to redefine emancipation in market terms" succinctly summarizes the point.[28] This is not to suggest that all criticisms of mainstream sexual rights movements, of sexual diversity policies, and of sexual modernization impulses are one and the same. As we have shown, these criticisms generally agree that sexual citizenship "has taken an overly accommodating stance on capital and social power"; but they are still divided as to whether a market-mediated emancipation is politically useful.[29]

Thus, while we tend to side with Fraser and therefore do not subscribe to the foregrounding of sexual freedom as necessarily politically transgressive,[30] we also believe that criticisms of sexual citizenship such as the ones we have reviewed offer too general a theory of sexuality under neoliberalism. They are too general in that they fail to show precisely *how* sexual identities, both marginal and hegemonic, may be subsumed under neoliberal capitalism. It is one thing to say that, once established, sexual citizenship is part of the citizenship of subjects in their dealings with both the state and the market. But it is another thing to suggest, as we do, that what needs to be explained is what people can do—and actually do—with these rights under the neoliberal condition.[31] In other words, it is not enough to understand how structural patterns of sexual inclusion and exclusion help sustain the capitalist system, either by legitimizing it or by expanding it through consumer culture. Rather, once we understand sexual rights as resources, the question immediately arises of how these resources are put to use or even realized by actual sexed citizens, be they queer or not.

Our alternative concept of neoliberal sexual capital builds on, but also goes beyond, the abstract idea that capitalism exploits emancipated and reclaimed collective sexual identities. The concept of sexual capital becomes useful precisely because it simultaneously acknowledges the (perceived) possibility for sexual freedom and the fact that, "as neoliberal rationality becomes our ubiquitous common sense," in the words of Wendy Brown,[32] individual liberty not only has become compatible with market freedom but is actually an extension of it.[33] Simply put, criticisms that merely point to the interchangeability between market and political freedoms miss the fact that neoliberal rationality has already altered the meaning of freedom. Wendy Brown again: "Instead, freedom is equated wholly with the pursuit of private ends, it is appropriately unregulated, and it is largely exercised to enhance the value, competitive positioning, or market share of a person or firm." Hence, what we need to account for is not just the commodification of sex and sexuality (which we still do: more on it later), but also how sexual freedom itself enhances the economic value of certain subjects.[34]

Finally, our concept of *neoliberal capital* departs from yet another set of arguments that criticize the commodification of sex and sexuality. In our previous discussion of sexual citizenship we foregrounded the political debate about market-mediated types of sexual inclusion and claims to rights. We now turn to explaining why critiques of consumer culture are insufficient to account for the contribution of sex and sexuality to the stronghold of neoliberal capitalism.

According to the thesis of the commodification of sex, the main problem with contemporary forms of sexuality is that, instead of liberating human beings, sexuality has become yet another realm conquered by capitalism. Simply put, critical theorists believe that, as part of modern capitalism's shift to consumption, a "desiring subject" has been formed and in this continuous process of releasing libidinous forces and of creating new consumer needs sex has become both a commodity and a means to sell other commodities.[35] Witness the panoply of commodities such as sex toys, erotic novels, or romantic getaways that are sold to consumers in various lifestyle markets.[36] As Ken Plummer suggests, there are five major "interlocking markets through which sexuality is consumed."[37] These are the market for sexualized "corporeal bodies" (e.g. sex tourism),[38] the market for sexual representations (e.g. pornography), the market for sexualized technologies (e.g. Viagra), the market for sexualized objects (e.g. sex toys), and, finally, the relationship market (e.g. Tantric sex workshops, seduction communities).

The sex industry has taken gigantic proportions. It generates billions in profits and bolsters corporations' revenues and national economies (the porn industry moved to internet platforms and is now integrated into digital capitalism). Sexual imagery permeates the public sphere, and this sexualization of culture bears significant social implications.[39] And yet, despite the centrality of these twin processes – the commodification of sex and the sexualization of culture – we argue that we should extend our account of the economic role of sex in society. While critical of the ever-expanding and visible processes of sexual commodification, we are more intrigued by sexual subjectivities and by actual sexual experiences and interactions than by sexual objects and commodities, no matter how increasingly central their role is in those interactions. Precisely because sex is so pervasive and visible, abundant and accessible, entangled in liberal ideals of personal authenticity and freedom but extremely commodified, sexual capital marks a complex system of differential capacities that add value to the self. We therefore ask: In a world of seeming sexual abundance, where all are supposed to have lots of good, pleasurable sex, could it also be that some can use sex to add more value to themselves, in the sense of increasing their market value? And, if this really is the case, then what would the cause be? Through the analytic prism of *sexual and erotic capital* we shall contribute to the sociological analysis of sexualities as a form of inequality, variously institutionalized in neoliberal capitalism. Instead of asking how capitalism reproduces heteronormative and gendered sexual scripts and narratives, we reverse the question, asking in what ways neoliberal sexuality and the sexual capital it may generate contribute to reproducing capitalism.

One way of addressing the structural principles of contemporary capitalism in western societies is to suggest, with Andreas Reckwitz, that "a social logic of singularities," markedly different from the previous modern social logic of generality, is on the rise since the 1980s.[40] We are no longer in the realm of mass-produced commodities. Instead, consumers prefer unique, artisanal, tailor-made options. The economic power of singularity also lies in the way capitalism taps into "life itself." Capitalism is absorbed into everyday life and devours all singularities. The result is that life becomes work (as in YouTube blogging, for example). Arguably, sex is a key site for both the enactment and the reproduction of the new social logic of singularity at work, both in subjectivities and in markets. Sex is normally regarded as a distinct episode in the routine of everyday life. Being a unique experience, sex is also normatively perceived as essentially non-utilitarian: it is an end in itself, be that procreation, pleasure maximization, or the maintenance of intimacy. Finally, due to its intrinsic value and uniqueness, sex is usually associated with strong affects such as "fascination, arousal, enthusiasm, and quiet satisfaction."[41]

We remain skeptic. In dealing with the contested terrain of neoliberal sexuality, we are less inclined to follow the invitation to generate a "joyful" sociological account of the singularity of sex.[42] We suggest instead that, although sex remains a key site for exercising gendered sexual scripts and for reproducing or transcending them (*pace* Hakim), sexual capital may also interact with class, but in ways that sociologists have yet to fully acknowledge. Sexual capital is operative in a social and political order that has been dubbed neoliberalism, a kind of throw-all notion that describes an increased responsibilization of the individual in the face of an increasingly deregulated market. To function optimally in the market, such a highly responsible individual must mobilize her or his psychic apparatus, sexual resources included. Over the past three decades, sociologists have insisted that class analysis must be reinvigorated, if we are to fully account for the perils of neoliberalization. Many analysts have suggested that class is not merely a structural and objective force coming from above. Crucially, they argue, class is also psychological, in that it works its way through subjectivity itself, in the experience of living in a body and having emotions. But looking at the role played by subjectivity in class formation and class reproduction is less developed. Notwithstanding, promising work in this direction is being currently done on artistic, creative, and cultural "passionate" occupations, where psychological investments are extremely pronounced. Recent studies have convincingly shown that middle-class creative workers see no outside to work. Thus, as work has become extremely precarious and unstable, demanding as it does workers' extreme readiness and aptness, it also functions as a deep expression of their authentic self.[43] Consequently, employability is conditioned precisely by that level of personal commitment and psychological, passionate investment. Michèle Lamont recently proposed that fostering self-worth, subjective well-being, and resilience may be one way to hamper the growing structural and material inequalities; and she suggested a link between the psychological and the social.[44] While we forcefully reject this psychological interpretation of inequalities, we want to assert that sex has become indeed a crucial site for cultivating feelings of self-worth, resilience, and aptness. This shift illustrates the ways in which the neoliberal self is called upon to exploit the totality of its skills and dimensions in order to enter and compete on the market. To put it differently, by looking at sexual capital we have a unique opportunity to understand how significant subjective experiences and psychological states are for (middle-class) employability and class reproduction. Emotional and sexual dispositions play an important role not only in strategies of social mobility but also in ways of defining oneself in the workplace.

Following a recent call by Breanne Fahs and Sara McClelland for greater conceptual clarity in the growing field of critical sexuality studies, in this short book we take it upon ourselves not only to offset the sexual capital metaphor but also to develop it further.[45] Thinking about sexual sensations, reactions, affects, bodies, identities, discourses, relationships, and commodities in terms of capital has the potential to explain the nuances and contradictions of sexual and social life under neoliberal capitalism. To exploit this potential, we shall problematize some of the more common and, avowedly, partial uses of the sexual capital metaphor and offer what we think are important corrections to this still highly useful way of thinking about sex and sexuality in present times. In this task we shall strive to be ambitious but modest.

Modest because, unlike some of the more well-known scholarly uses of the concept of sexual capital, our own formulation of this metaphor is more realistic. Our *ambitiousness*, on the other hand, is grounded in an attempt to gain a better understanding of how "sex and power collide"[46] by taking into account the class mechanism behind the unequal distribution of sexual capital. In the latter part of the book we thus argue that sexual capital has also become a factor in the reproduction of class hierarchies.

We will start with an overview of the historical transition from modern to late modern formations of sex and sexuality. In this transition, the modern division between 'good sex', which belongs to the sphere of reproduction, and 'bad sex', that is, commercial sex, has eroded. The shift lays the historical ground for explaining how sex produces economic capital—either directly, in the form of sexual commodities and services, or indirectly, through mating practices and by creating subjects and subjectivities. This theoretical and historical review allows us to develop the notion of neoliberal sexual capital, whereby the employability of workers is enhanced through their personal sexual experiences.

2

Sexual Freedom and Sexual Capital

All human beings have a sex, yet not all of them have a sexuality, that is, the view that their sexual organs define them and their actions and have an importance for the flourishing of the self. Sexuality has profoundly redefined identity and selfhood in modernity. We may thus ask, with scholars: How have we come to believe that sex is so important to who we are? We modern people think that sex and sexuality are a natural drive and appetite[1] that must be cultivated and practiced for itself, for the well-being of the body and psyche. Sexuality has condensed the value and practice of freedom or, more precisely, of personal freedom. The association between personal autonomy and self-realization on the one hand, sexual liberty on the other is the outcome of a long socio-historical process. Indeed, sexual freedom has become a central principle of modern western society and one of the most striking legacies of the Enlightenment, whose consequences "are unfolding still."[2] Sociologist Adam Isaiah Green follows this line of thinking when he writes:

> in the last two centuries, broad structural shifts related to the growth of capitalist markets, urbanization and the changing socioeconomic status of women have coincided with technological and cultural developments—including the advent of birth control, the popularity of the internet, the waning influence of religion, and the rise of sex-positive norms—to produce a domain of sexual life ever more free from traditional institutions of control, such as the family and the church.[3]

Sexual freedom, then, is a set of ideas, a matrix of values, a cultural frame, and a practice that has had a powerful impact on modern institutions and relations, intimate and economic alike.

In the highly influential writings of Michel Foucault, sexual freedom is viewed as an effect of new forms of knowledge about the self (provided by psychiatry and psychoanalysis most noticeably). But, as Eva Illouz has argued, both the idea and the practice of sexual freedom have espoused the main social forms and logic of consumer capitalism.[4] Perhaps because Michel Foucault was concerned to distinguish himself from Marxism, he focused on the knowledge systems about sexuality and was oblivious to the gigantic economic underpinnings of sexuality and to the sexualization of the economy. Sexual freedom was incorporated into economic and social fields and morphed into a kind of capital—an unevenly distributed resource that yielded various types of advantages in different socio-historical circumstances. We ask: What are the various forms of capital that the modern ideal of sexual liberalization takes? And how does the metaphor of sexual capital capture these changing forms?

Modern sexuality is characterized by a dual process: sex becomes rationalized and objectified in scientific bodies of knowledge; and sex becomes a personal attribute, an identity, and hence a property of the person, individual and private, an aspect of one's core identity. We may theorize this historical process in terms of a supposed gradual autonomization of sex as a relatively distinct sphere of human action; this would be quite similar to how Pierre Bourdieu described the emergence of the literary and other artistic fields.[5] A good illustration of this kind of modern imaginary of sex can be found in Max Weber's description of "the erotic sphere," one of six spheres of value he posited. According to Weber, the gradual sublimation of sex went hand in hand with the growing rationalization and intellectualization of the modern world. Sex thus became a safe haven in an otherwise cold world:

> It occurred where this sphere collided with the unavoidably ascetic trait of the specialist. Under this tension between the erotic sphere and rational everyday life, specifically extramarital sexual life, which had been removed from everyday affairs, could appear as the only tie which still linked man with the natural fountain of all life. For man had now been completely emancipated from the cycle of the old, simple and organic existence of the peasant.[6]

For Weber, the "joyous triumph over rationality" that sex enables can culminate either in innerwordly "pure animality" or, potentially, in an otherworldly ethical salvation from rationality through "boundless giving of oneself."[7] In this way, eroticism potentially relieves men—and, to a lesser extent, women—of their rationalist endeavors and counters the coldness of capitalist calculation. For Weber, and in some respects for Georg Simmel too, sex is an "assertion of self against the preternaturally distorting effects of modern and later industrial civilization."[8] Weber thus contextualized the purification of the erotic and its separation from everyday brute life, treating the erotic as a shield from the cold bureaucratization that came with rationalized capitalist development. The satisfaction of "men's" (and presumably women's) sexual desire is detached from any other interests besides its own. Thus, although sex remains suspicious enough for Weber (and for the other sociological "fathers" as well),[9] importantly, it is now understood sociologically as constituting a sphere of action of its own, one likely to grow in importance with modernity.

Now, if we assume that there has been an actual historical process of sexual autonomization, then the question that interests us is what the social implications of this process are. If both society at large and sociologists increasingly conceive of sex as an end in itself and as having some intrinsic value, where exactly does that value emanate from? While Weber thought of eroticism as a sphere that yields pleasure, we think of such an autonomization of sexuality as yielding even more benefits.

Pace Weber, scholars who documented the emergence of an autonomous sexual field in society have mainly explained it by resorting to post-traditionalism and advanced capitalism.[10] One important way in which sociologists have tackled sexual autonomization was to look at the transformation of the social arrangements that regulated romantic love and marital bonds. In *Why Love Hurts* Eva Illouz describes a process parallel to the one Weber described.[11] With modernity, she argues, a "great transformation of love" occurred that has given rise to self-regulating modern marriage markets. What this means is that the taboos of race and religion that controlled the rules of exogamy (i.e. mate choice) weakened considerably, while the "utility" of a partner of choice came to be associated not only with his or her social–economic standing, like before, but also with psychological, emotional, and sexual attributes. Partner choice was increasingly based on sexual desirability and psychological compatibility.

The bourgeois society of industrial capitalism made sex both an object of study and a site of personal identity. Sexuality was increasingly understood, imagined, and discussed as a non-monetized entity removed from the economic market, even if not entirely autonomous, as in Weber. Proper, "good" sex was considered to be domestic and to belong to the sphere of biological and social reproduction (which is what the family stood for). The normative assumption was that sex and the economy should be, or actually are, separate from each other. Interestingly, later on, during what is known as the sexual revolution of the 1920s (the first), these same ideals were criticized by various social reformist groups and thinkers. Some of them believed that the domestication of sex was the mark of a repressive bourgeois morality. In this respect, they reconnected sex—now discursively framed as "repressed"—and the capitalist mode of production. A good example of such a way of thinking can be found in Werner Sombart, who wrote in 1913 that the petit bourgeois is chaste because "he does not want to jeopardize his whole existence . . . he must arrive at the conclusion that the contracture of debts and the wasting of his time in amusements and love affairs will reduce him to beggary."[12] While sexual "repressiveness" was viewed as serving the interests of capitalism (a theme later invoked by Herbert Marcuse in his critique of the one-dimensional man),[13] another process was slowly taking place: it was one in which sexual liberation would serve the interests of capitalism far more directly.

* * *

Sociologists and other sex researchers employ the concept of sexual capital to explain how sexual subjectivities, experiences, and interactions— including actions, feelings, and thoughts—are used by social agents to their advantage, be it in economic markets, in marriage markets, or in sexual encounters.

We try to connect sexual capital to class and gender relations and view sexual capital as a way to gain status and acquire economic benefits. We thereby join a recent trend to reengage with material inequalities through what Andrew Sayer calls "a radical political economy." A radical and moral political economy is not "limited to matters of equality and exploitation" but has a strong sense of "economic responsibilities" and of "the public good."[14] Thomas Piketty's work would be one obvious recent example of such a "return to [the] scrutiny of material realities."[15] However, one shortcoming of this otherwise welcome approach is that it largely discards non-economic definitions of capital.[16] We, on the other hand, extend and expand the notion of capital and employ non-economic, "unpurified" versions of it in the study of material and gender inequalities.[17] We believe that an expanded capital-based approach is perfectly suited to reveal the ways in which sexualities and inequalities are currently linked together. This is because, as Andrew Sayer argues,[18] a revived radical political economy needs to investigate how markets, money, and capital intrude and distort lifeworlds. In the last chapter of this book we develop the idea that neoliberal sexual capital is a specific path through which material inequalities persist. But before delving into our typology of the four forms of sexual capital we offer a short introduction to the general idea of sexual capital.

3

What Is Sexual Capital?

As argued so far, there are many ways to address the notion of sexual capital. The four categories of sexual capital that we are about to discuss differ in how they configure both the "sexual" and the "capital" components of the term. Hence, before presenting these categories, we will define the key notions of sex and capital that stand behind the two components.

Sex

As sex historian Valerie Traub insists, it must be acknowledged that sex as "a category of human thought, volition, behavior and representation is opaque, inaccessible and resistant to understanding."[1] It is hard to determine what sex is and what sex is not. This is why, Traub goes on to claim, historians and, we may add, sociologists have rarely described the physical contents of sex.[2] For us, the realm of sexual experience is a continuum that runs from desire through actual sexual behaviors, acts, and competences to what counts as public identities.[3] In our typology, "the sexual" designates two very broad human terrains of action. First, it refers quite generally to the sexiness and attractiveness of bodies, the property that makes them desirable to others.[4] There are whole industries (plastic surgery, sexy lingerie, fitness, etc.) designed to make a person feel and appear more attractive in order to have more sexual success. Being recognized as sexy or beautiful may enlarge one's sexual popularity and bring about pleasure maximization. The second broad referent of "the sexual" is the realm of sexual experience and expression, and this includes "everything that turns us on."[5] In reality, the two referents are of course intimately linked.[6] Nevertheless, they need to be analytically separated.

The sexual capital metaphor was first developed in the context of a research carried out on LGBTQ communities and sexual subcultures,[7] but it makes perfect sense to apply it to heterosexual relations as well. In the past few decades the constructed and contingent nature of heterosexuality became even more obvious, as multiple forms of pairings and sexual arrangements emerged.[8] But heterosexuality still remains highly institutionalized and demands endless cultural work devoted to reaffirming its normativity.[9] Hence, even if our discussion is relevant to queer sexuality, we focus on heterosexuality, because heterosexuality retains much of its past moral characteristics even as they become gradually destabilized; remains less politicized in social space than other types of sexual relating; and is generally experienced as natural and private. Finally, heterosexuality is the form of sexuality that yields the most obvious and tangible forms of capital.

Capital

What do we mean by "capital"? In the first volume of *Das Kapital*, Karl Marx asserts that (economic) capital is the appropriation of surplus value—the exploited labor of others—as well as the circulation of this surplus value back into the production sphere.[10] In this formulation, "capital is a quantity of goods or money which, when exchanged for labor, reproduces and augments itself by extracting unpaid labor, or surplus value, from labor and into itself."[11] This is already a much expanded and fluid view on capital insofar as it separates capital from value. Marx's capital "moves through three different forms, those of money, productive and commodity capital. Associated with each of these forms, a particular corresponding understanding of capital is encouraged—as finance, an instrument of production, or output that embodies a surplus over inputs."[12] Thus Marx accepts—but also goes beyond—the original, purely monetized meaning of capital. According to Geoffrey Hodgson, the original meaning was purely economic, but it gradually expanded, and it now (unjustifiably, according to him) includes non-economic types of capital as well.[13] From the original, minimalist meaning, which referred only "to money, or the money value of alienable property,"[14] political economists such as Adam Smith or Karl Marx and sociologists such as Pierre Bourdieu offered to extend the definition to any resource that "can help in the production of wealth,"[15] either economic or social.

Other expanded theorizations of capital shun the labor theory of value and the working class and shift the focus instead to the middle classes and to various composites of economic proxies such as education credentials and professional or technical skills, also known as human capital, that generate occupational advantages for these classes.[16] Finally, we are particularly influenced by Bourdieu's field theory as well as by the cultural turn when we suggest that capital can be non-economic, as in cultural and social capitals.[17] Such forms of capital have been extended; thus Illouz proposes the notion of emotional capital, which deals with how emotions are shaped, trained, and expressed as a way to compete in the workplace, and Lamont proposes the notion of moral capital, which shows us how the moral designation of self and others marks someone in a field.[18]

Hodgson summarizes the expanded or all-encompassing meaning of capital as he critically asserts that, by the 1970s, the term "capital" began to be applied to almost any durable object, property, personal attribute, or social relationship that could be economically useful—to the point that, he claims, "capital" lost its explanatory power.[19] Despite this critique, we adopt the expansive approach, in which the meaning of capital extends beyond the purely monetary sphere to (seemingly) non-economic realms of accumulation and investment such as that of sexual experience. Indeed, this analytical move is important for our discussion of sexual capital, which perceives the sexual realm as being integral to social—*and* economic—inequalities, albeit not entirely reducible to them.

The first reason why we extend the notion of "capital" is purely definitional. As recent studies have shown, even within the discipline of economics itself, there is no consensus over the meaning of "capital." In their intellectual history of modern economic thought on capital, economists Anthony Endres and David Harper make the point that at different times economists have metaphorized "capital" differently.[20] Throughout the twentieth century, new and divergent ways of theorizing and understanding the term were found, and each one carried with it different ontological assumptions as to the nature of (the economic) reality. But beyond the lack of disciplinary consensus among economists over the meaning of "capital," our second reason for expanding the concept beyond monetary and explicitly economic realms is analytic. Economic and sociological metaphors bring to the fore *certain* aspects of the economic and the social reality, whereas other aspects move to the back. *This is precisely why we need an extended notion of capital*: different types of capital correspond to different forms of inequality and to the different social modes of accumulating (or not) the social advantages that these social inequalities generate in the first place.[21] For Laurent Thévenot, "[t]he diversification of capital variables does not simply add other types of capital." Rather, the many forms of capital shed light on

> the irreducible heterogeneity of the ways in which people are able to "capitalize" their assets and valorize their capital, a diversity that I characterize as "modes of coordination" with others, with oneself, and with the surrounding world. There is no "return on investment" without an appropriate mode of coordination, determining a particular mode of valorization of capital.[22]

As already noted, one of the most researched modes of coordination in sociology is the one related to the accrual of cultural capital and to the social advantages it generates for the middle and upper classes. The extensive research on cultural capital, developed mostly in the sociology of culture and in the sociology of education, demonstrates that the stocks of meanings and capacities acquired in early socialization through family practices shape subsequent outcomes in the educational system and, later, in employment markets.[23] Cultural capital continues to shape adult life in the form of class-specific consumer and lifestyle tastes, and these distinct tastes then operate as signals of status and propriety.[24] The other forms of capital developed by Bourdieu and by other sociologists who followed this sociological reasoning are similarly embedded in their own specific social fields and corresponding modes of coordination. By expanding the meaning of capital beyond monetary investment and returns in the economic field alone, sociologists have been able to offer a more nuanced approach to how various types of structural inequalities operate together, sometimes overlapping, sometimes merely reinforcing each other.[25]

Sexual capital

This brings us to the question of how to conceive of sexual capital. What kinds of advantages may the stock of embodied and individually owned sexual capacities produce? Are these advantages merely sexual, or can sexual assets yield non-sexual advantages, too? And, if they can, are these advantages translatable into the economic sphere, as some sociologists inspired by Bourdieu's work on symbolic capital would suggest?[26] Under what conditions can sexual capital become economically valuable? To answer this set of questions, the next chapter is premised on the common distinction between two arenas for the coordination of sexual capital: the economic sphere of *production* and labor relations; and the domestic sphere of *reproduction* (category 1 of sexual capital). However, as we shall see, in moving from *sexual capital as surplus value of the body* (category 2) to sexiness and *embodied sexual capital* (category 3), it will hopefully become clear that it is harder to maintain distinction between production and reproduction, not only ideologically (as many feminists have already argued)[27] but also ontologically, simply because neoliberal capitalism blurs the two spheres. In present times, the analytical separation between the spheres of material production and social reproduction cannot be easily retained. Rather we are confronted with a sexual world in which it becomes harder to distinguish sex work from domestic "gift" sex and from other forms of labor. These transformations constitute the broader context in which *neoliberal sexual capital* (category 4) emerges.

4

Forms of Sexual Capital

The Four Categories

We now turn to our typology of four different forms of sexual capital. This typology is partly historical, partly analytical. Here we are influenced by Nancy Fraser's historical–analytical move, according to which during every historical capitalist stage the unlimited forces of accumulation periodically come into tension and often destabilize practices of social reproduction.[1] The actual historical manifestations of this contradiction vary, but their source is unchanged and is rooted in the capitalist structure of society. Thus, each category of sexual capital should be seen as manifesting the historically specific shape of the tension between the reproduction of social life and the accumulation of capital.

We identify four ideal types of sexual capital and specify how they are used and exchanged in social and economic relationships. The four categories are:

1. *Sexual capital by default: Chastity and domesticity.* Here a person's reputation is denigrated in a marriage market if she "loses" her virginity. Chastity (lack of sexual activity) thus plays the role of positive sexual capital, what makes a woman attractive on the marriage market. Chastity is, historically, the first indication that sexuality is marked as a social value, even if in the mode of its negation. Chastity functions as capital in a society governed by religious patriarchies. It shows the ways in which the body of women is marked and controlled by men and the ways in which this moral value can be converted into the economic asset that marriage represents in traditional societies.

2. *Sexual capital as surplus value of the body.* This category is to be found in the capacity to make the sexual body into a commodity, as in prostitution and other forms of sex work. Prostitution exists in traditional societies and extends to contemporary sex industries. Here

the monetization of sexuality is direct and explicit. Sex is exchanged for money. We may even speak of a commodification of sexual services (as when different forms of sexual interaction are differently charged, in other words have different monetary values).

3. *Embodied sexual capital.* This form of capital is more indirect and refers to the fact that, under the aegis of what Illouz has called scopic capitalism, a large set of industries extract surplus value from the sexualized body and the sexual self.[2] This basically means that "sex sells" not only within the sex industry itself, but also in cultural images and productions. This value or capital extends to the realm of relationships, since sexual attractiveness and sexual know-how become crucial to the ability to form and maintain them. The phenomenon of incels—involuntary celibates—suggests that some people may fall on the wayside of such markets.

4. *Neoliberal sexual capital.* This form of capital is the innovation of our study. It designates the fact that, for many people, some sexual recreation may translate into a feeling of social competence, self-efficacy, and self-

appreciation that can in turn feed into a proactive and entrepreneurial stance sought by employers. As we will explain, this form of sexual capital has emerged as distinctively late modern, and we therefore dub it "neoliberal sexual capital."

Before we elaborate on the four categories of sexual capital, a brief historical survey of the moral economy of modern sexuality is in place. This overview demonstrates two things in particular. First, while sex and sexuality have always been embedded in the economic sphere (and this is true of marriage markets as much as it is of sex work), such embeddedness—the fact that sex and sexuality are not outside capitalism—is not always intelligible to contemporaries (as we have seen in Weber).[3] Secondly, as we progress in time, the moral condemnation of the embeddedness of sex in the economic sphere tends to wane. Specifically, with the characteristically neoliberal collapse of the boundaries between the realms of work and non-work, the exchange value of sex and of sexiness is more publicly acknowledged and socially acceptable than it used to be in the past.[4] Obviously, this does not mean that most women (or men) would now actively choose to become sex workers, for instance. But there are indications that phenomena like soft prostitution are spreading to parts of the middle class and that not all sex workers are necessarily devalued and lack self-appreciation.[5] One informant told Joanna Brewis and Stephen Linstead:

> I like being a sex worker because I am a member of an elite group of multi-talented professional workers. I am at different times a lover, psychiatrist, teacher, counsellor, educator, masseuse, therapist and sometimes all of these at once. I like role playing . . . I like that I am helping to lessen the loneliness of the many clients who see me. Some of these men are widowers, some find it difficult to sustain relationships, some have never had a relationship. It makes me feel good to share an intimate experience with these men that is warm, sensual and caring and hopefully they will carry some of that experience away with them.[6]

Here sex work becomes a professional occupation of a therapeutic nature, which suggests the gradual entry of sexualized forms of labor to the legitimate labor market. How has the essentially private, non-monetized *singularity* of sexual experiences been incorporated into the neoliberal labor process to create neoliberal sexual capital (our fourth category)?

In what follows we try to answer this question by foregrounding three dimensions in particular. The first dimension is the *location of sex*. Here the question is whether sex is perceived as belonging to the sphere of production and having an exchange value or whether it is perceived as belonging to the private sphere and being a non-work activity with use value only. In dealing with this dimension we draw on both feminist and queer theories and terminologies. The second dimension we consider here is the *gendered nature of sex*: the fact that sex is scripted and experienced through inscribed gender norms and habitus. The third dimension is the *particular terrain of sexual action*, that is, either the external attractiveness of a sexual body or the realm of intrinsic sexual experience.

Locating modern gendered sex: "Good" reproduction and "bad" production?

With the rise of modernity, the idea that domestic sexuality is—and should be—separated from the capitalist system became widely accepted. As we have already seen in Weber, sexual relations were understood as potentially counterbalancing the instrumental rationality that came along with modern commerce. This was "good" sex (specifically if it was marital). But there was also "bad" sex, running the whole gamut from prostitution to mercenary marriage.[7] In this respect, sex and sexuality were perceived as potentially constructive *and* disruptive to the social body, as pleasurable *and* dangerous. This picture is already very different from the one associated with the early modern figure of Don Juan, discussed in chapter 1, and with the religious threats that the fictional figure posed to the moral order of society in that era. Instead, according to the modern moral social order, for *some* people sexual interactions are merely transactional, whereas for others sex is a social relation based on intimacy and love. As we will show in greater detail here, the determining factor is the locus of the interaction.[8] Is the sexual encounter located in the sphere of production, as a fleeting market exchange? Or is it part of a future-oriented and emotionally bound relationship, placed in the domestic sphere and perceived as contributing to the social reproduction of society?

To a great extent, the bifurcation into good and bad sex was premised on liberal beliefs that spiritual and material growth are incommensurable. Market interestedness relies upon the existence of disinterested spheres of activity (spiritual, artistic, intimate).[9] Hence this perspective compartmentalized socio-sexual life into the two supposedly separate realms of production and reproduction.[10] Apparently, then, in modernity bad commercial sex and "good" domestic sex co-produced each other. This relational antinomy is nicely put in Gayle Rubin's sex hierarchy diagrams.[11] As Rubin shows, monogamous, heterosexual, relationship-based, and non-commercial sex has been culturally set against non-normative sex such as homosexual or, more relevant to our argument, commercial sex.

Unlike domestic sex, commercial sex produces direct monetary capital, as in prostitution and other forms of sex work. This is one important reason why commercial sex was (and to a great extent still is) deemed morally dubious. Here capital is generated through sexualized labor, the actual sexual services that, in most cases, men purchase from women. To be sure, the global political economy of the commercial sex trade

49

has changed in significant ways since the 1960s.[12] In its present, corporatized state, it is certainly not comparable to what it was in the nineteenth century, or even the first half of the twentieth. But, in both modern and late modern societies, the sexual labor of sex workers creates monetary capital.

But the good sex–bad sex antinomy did more than just oppose the two sexual moralities. The normative modern relegation of good sex to the sphere of reproduction and affectionate social relationships not only situated sex as the opposite of utilitarian commerce and of self-interested behaviors. It also placed sex and sexuality in a causal, structural relationship with the economic functioning of societies. Interestingly, some contemporary writers discussed sex as a prism through which to contemplate societal changes and capitalist progress. Inspecting the intersections between sex and the developing commercial economy, the eighteenth-century political economist Bernard Mandeville famously pointed out the compatibility, as he saw it, of private (sexual) vices and self-interest with the common good of economic development.[13] Although he believed that prostitution is a vice, he nevertheless suggested that regulated prostitution was useful to both business and the modesty of virtuous women who belonged to the civil society.[14] Gradually Mandeville's ideas on the significance of private sexual fulfillment for the smooth functioning of capitalist production became culturally prominent. By the beginning of the twentieth century, the notion that a rationalized good sexuality could foster economic production became quite prominent. According to this mode of thinking, good sex virtually supported capitalist production. Here the sphere of reproduction

> is not only meant to complement that of the market, that is, to supplement what market relations can deliver; more than just a safety net, it is required for the formation of subjects who can distinguish between the negotiable and the inalienable and may expect to be treated according to this distinction.[15]

In such a formulation sex becomes important to capitalist production precisely because it belongs to the non-market sphere of reproduction, where subjects are cultivated, nurtured, and reproduced, in short, where they are made full-fledged subjects.

That sex and sexuality produce value for capital not only through market transactions but in the private sphere as well has been the subject of sustained and elaborate feminist critique. According to this line of argument, the economic dependency of women enables the exploitation of their sexual, reproductive, and emotional labor and, more broadly, the functioning and prolongation of patriarchic capitalism.[16] Thus the regulation of sexuality within the bounds of procreational and, later, romantic or relational heterosexuality has been key to the capitalist mode of production and to capital accumulation.[17] Indeed, Antonio Gramsci, like Sigmund Freud before him, believed that, in order to work properly, men must lead a fulfilling private sex life.[18] This led feminist scholars to argue that the "process of reproduction of labor-power/sexuality in our societies occurs at the expense of women and their labor."[19]

According to this view, women alienate their sexual capacities and use their looks or the sexual parts of their bodies in a way that produces surplus value and capital either for the sex industry or, more broadly, for society, in the form of biological reproduction.[20] This is not to collapse the fundamental differences between the sex industry and the domestic sphere. Still, in most of the cases that fall under the category we dub "sexual capital as surplus value of the body" (our category 2), economic capital is produced through men's exploitation of women's "means of sexuality."[21] Arguably, this is what triggered Catherine Hakim's plea that women reverse this logic and capitalize on their sexual assets in the legitimate labor market rather than limit to the domestic sphere their sexual encounters (or "exchanges") with men.[22]

Another way to historicize sexual capital through the tridimensional lens of location, gender, and the sexual is by opting for a completely different research tradition, which focuses on the sexual status and the internal hierarchies of desirability upheld by those who participate in various sexual "fields" or subcultures, such as gay bars, speed dating, or Tinder encounters.[23] Sexual fields may span a "punk nightclub in New York City,"[24] an urban gay village, or an entire nation.[25] For example, Tom Inglis discusses Irish sexuality as a field in its own right.[26] This research tradition started in the 1930s, in the context of American college dating systems functioning as marriage markets,[27] but it is now applied mostly to casual sex encounters.

According to the sexual fields approach, certain social actors enjoy more sexual capital than others. This means that they are better placed to have sex with appealing people and to see their status increase as a result.[28] Sexual status competitions of this sort are based on collective schemes of evaluating sexual attractiveness that are shared by participants in a given field. Value judgments can be quite specific, as we find in the "bear" subculture of the queer community, or much wider, as demonstrated by Martin Weinberg and Colin Williams in their study of a San Francisco transgender bar.[29] Weinberg and Williams found that Asian trans women were considred by male patrons to be the most attractive ones, because their gender performances were perceived as being the most feminine. Similarly, Green shows that, in a largely middle-class and white sexual community in Manhattan, some black gay men who performed hegemonic masculinities enjoyed sexual success, but were not very desirable when it came to long-term relationships.[30] A final example of such sexual capital can be found in Ashley Mears' study of an international party circuit in which tall, slender, and especially pretty young women (usually not older than twenty-five) meet very rich men in clubs known as "whales," where bottles and food are particularly expensive. Unattractive women are excluded from such clubs.[31] The high-quality crowd gathered in these milieus consists first and foremost of "models or women who look like models"—given that models stand at the top of the hierarchy created by the social field in which sexual capital is at stake. This type of environment generates new forms of economic activity and status, for example men whose (fuzzy) activity consists in bringing rich men together with beautiful young women, creating networks, and drawing to themselves the prestige associated with proximity to beauty and money. At first sight, this seems to place sex in the reproductive sphere, for partners meet solely for the sake of pleasure and with the aim of nurturing their sexual status. However, sexual fields are also part of the "relationship market"[32] and elaborate industries form around them, as in the case of "seduction communities."[33]

Lastly, "neoliberal sexual capital" designates the economic value that subjects may derive from their own sexual qualities, capacities, and experiences. At first sight this category might seem similar to those of Hakim and other "sexual economics" scholars,[34] and in some respects it is. Yet neoliberal sexual capital differs from rational choice formulations of erotic capital such as Hakim's or Baumeister et al.'s, according to whom sex is an essentially female resource that gets exchanged with men's valuable assets. We suggest instead that it would be more useful to think of neoliberal sexual capital in class terms as well as in gender terms.[35] This form of capital is less directly gendered, because "sex" does not refer here either to reproduction and kinship or to sexiness, two areas that are still considered almost exclusively relevant to women. Neoliberal sexual capital does not entirely concern hierarchies of erotic desirability in society and the ensuing exchange systems (e.g. situations where women "sell" their sexual charms in return for men's nonmaterial assets).[36] We see this form of sexual capital (our category 4) rather as a variant of human capital.[37] This means that one's sex life—her sexual experiences, affects, and desires—may enhance middle-class employability.[38] Neoliberal sexual capital does not use sexiness (the sexual affects induced by one body in another's). Rather than erotic attractiveness, this kind of capital uses the singular quality of sexual experiences, the fact that we experience sex at a purely subjective level, as a way of forming a self that is entirely compatible with the skills and properties that define social and professional competence at large. This sexual capital is inscribed in general strategies of learning about oneself, of cultivating confidence and self-esteem, of taking risks, and mostly, perhaps, of managing relationships through self-assertion and dominance. In other words, neoliberal sexual capital, we propose, may generate advantages that are obtained in the sexual arena but may go well beyond it. Middle-class subjects are more inclined than others to glean self-appreciation from their sex life and are, moreover, better positioned to use their sexual capital in their professional life.[39] As we shall demonstrate, this does not mean that neoliberal sexual capital operates the same way for men and women. But, while some practices associated with the accumulation of sexual capital seem to be divided by gender (sex parties for high-tech Silicon Valley male elites, polyamorous relationships for women and their partners), this does not change the basic path: sexual experiences in the private sphere become useful in the production sphere not as sex work, but as completely "normal" professional settings.

Historically, this form of sexual capital has emerged in late modernity, when the sphere of economic production and employment became increasingly enmeshed with the sphere of social reproduction (sex, sexuality, families, and intimate relationships).[40] We conclude by proposing that neoliberal sexual capital not only is shaped by neoliberal capitalism but also legitimizes it and advances it still further.

Looking more closely at the analytical framework outlined so far, we offer four categories: sexual capital by default, sexual capital as surplus value of the body, embodied sexual capital, and neoliberal sexual capital as enhancement of workers' employability.

Sexual capital by default: Chastity and domesticity

The normative bifurcation into good and bad sex discussed so far tapped into a particular set of assumptions about gender roles. As Faramerz Dabhoiwala argues, "the Enlightenment reconfiguration of masculinity and femininity gave rise to some of the thorniest social and ethical questions of the modern sexual world. . . . How ought men and women to behave?"[41] As many have argued, by the end of the eighteenth century the general attitude toward the sexuality of men and women started to undergo a very significant transformation.[42] Women were desexualized, as it came to be widely believed that they were naturally, innately, and scientifically the chaster sex (and therefore morally superior to men). They held a kind of sexual capital by default that encapsulated two gender ideologies. First was the ideology that separated moral from immoral women through the dimension of money—that is, the venality of women. Patriarchy shaped by Christian ideals of sexual abstention separated chaste from unchaste women and sex for money from sex for reproduction in the legitimate framework of marriage. Secondly, there was the ideology that all women are by nature virginal, sexually tame, and even passionless.[43] Culturally coded this way, chastity operated as a sign of class and morality, and thus could be used as capital in the bourgeois marriage markets of the eighteenth and nineteenth centuries. In return for their chaste sexual morality, bourgeois women gained economic security through marriage, practicing reproduction rather than sex for pleasure; the latter, by analogy with a one-time monetary transaction, was traded for long-term economic status. In this strict gendered moral economy, sexual capital by default maintained the ideal that all "good" women—as opposed to those who had "fallen"—were chaste until proven otherwise. Sexual chastity was morally boosted by the fact that the economic character of the transaction was not perceived as venal.

This "clean" story is, of course, much more historically nuanced, not only in terms of gender but also in terms of class, race, and locale. As gender historian Hera Cook suggests, major changes in sexual activity had occurred during the nineteenth century.[44] During the early eighteenth century, many plebeian English women were engaged in casual sexual practices. Owing to community pressures, men (and women) were forced to take responsibility for their offspring, and this resulted in long-term stability even for non-married couples. Yet by the nineteenth century working and living patterns had considerably changed with the rise of urbanization, factory work, and waged labor. Capitalism made working-class women more dependent on men and thereby sexually more vulnerable. Legal marriage thus came to be very much sought after by women—but not without a price:

> When women cannot support themselves and their children by their own labour then marriage or cohabitation becomes their trade. In such a society men can demand female subordination, and a successful wife will ensure she does not threaten her security by unwanted boldness, flirtatiousness, or displays of sexual knowledge. Thus there is a strong link between women's economic autonomy and their sexual behavior.[45]

In the absence of birth control, the economic insecurity of working-class and poor women, together with the growing middle classes' moral, religious, and political powers, gradually made sexual respectability hegemonic. Victorian discourses and beliefs on sexuality were strongly related to religion, fostering ideals of sexual restraint and self-control.

But by the twentieth century it had become more widely acknowledged that ("normal") sexual expression and satisfaction are key to any successful marriage, to selfhood, and even to social competence at large.[46] In fact marital sexual satisfaction became a social problem, at least for the respectable middle classes. If chaste women lacked sexual experience, many middle-class and upper-middle-class men were sexually socialized in the climate of commercial sex, where they were not required to be intimate and considerate.[47] This reality prompted Freud to suggest, in his essay "'Civilized' Sexual Morality and Modern Nervous Illness," that the marital bed was an unhappy one: men were rarely potent, women were often frigid. In such a state of sexual emergency, it was not only the happiness of individual women and men that was at stake, but the fate of society. This also meant that the commercialization of sex and morality stood at opposite ends of the social spectrum. Prostitutes, working-class women who looked for favors from men, and women who belonged to the *demi-monde* (such as actresses) were all integrated into an economic circuit in which sexual favors were exchanged for money, while respectable women executed their role inside a domestic unit, thus keeping at bay the danger that sexuality posed to their moral standing.

Sex can be socially redeeming not only because it helps bourgeois men be productive members of society, as Freud suggested.[48] It also ensures that the petit bourgeois shopkeeper is thrifty, as we have already seen in Werner Sombart.[49] Good, marital sex also turned the working class into more efficient and docile workers, as the carmaker Henry Ford intimated to his workers.[50] Thus sexual repression, some contemporaries believed, was necessary for capitalism. It was precisely this connection between the rationalized sexuality of economic subjects of varying standings and their docility and usefulness to capital accumulation that drove some 1920s German and American social revolutionaries and progressives to suggest that a sexual revolution was much needed.

But even then, when sexual fulfillment in the home was recognized as important for capitalist production, chastity continued to play an enormous part in women's life even after they got married. Lisa Pruitt studied the legal history of female defamation plaintiffs in the United States, where women have sought legal redress for statements about their supposed unchaste sexual behavior. Pruitt argues that until the turn of the twentieth century women were anxious to safeguard their sexual reputation as truly private persons, within their small social circle: "She typically functioned entirely within the domestic sphere of life, apart from the commercial marketplace, and it was the impact of the offending statement on these 'private relationships' that constituted her injury."[51] Around the turn of the century, Pruitt argues, courts increasingly recognized the interrelation between private and public and treated sexual slanders as potentially compromising to women's employability, too. This is an example of how sexual chastity, through reputation, played a role in marriageability and employability.

Sexual capital as surplus value of the body

Some aspects of labor are remunerated for the sexual services they provide. Such forms of labor occur (mostly) within the sex industry, which includes prostitution, pornography, and erotic dancing.[52] In 1970, the total market of "hardcore pornography," meaning explicit depictions of sexual intercourse, was estimated somewhere between $5 million and $10 million.[53] In 1996, the journalist Eric Schlosser evaluated that Americans had spent $8 billion on porn, sex magazines, and the like.[54] In 2018, a reasonable guess at this industry's revenues outs them between $6 billion and $15 billion.[55] According to the internet platform Pornhub, in 2019 the website had more than 42 billion visits, meaning that on average it had 115 million visits a day.[56]

The sex industry is extremely multifaceted, and so is the scholarship about it. Our intention is neither to rehearse the main lines of argument in this scholarly field nor to challenge the gravity of the human, political, economic, and social implications for most of those who sell their sexual labor power on the sex market. Instead, we want to direct attention to what we think is a slight shift both in the societal norms that govern sex work and in how some sex workers come to experience it.

As we noted earlier, in modernity the exchange of money has been the threshold that separates good sex from bad. In this social imaginary, sex is socially acceptable and even encouraged, either for the sake of intimate relations and procreation or, lately, for recreational purposes only, as casual sex, as long as it is (seemingly) located outside the matrix of capital. By contrast, directly monetized sex is bad. Thus, if the body is the main vector through which capital is accumulated,[57] then, as many have already stressed, the crudest and most direct forms of monetary sexual capital are the ones accrued through prostitution—that is, through the exploitation of the sexual labor power of typically vulnerable women, men, and children in poverty.[58]

Yet in recent times good sex has become so commodified and valuable in so many "interlocking markets"[59] that the hard-wired modernist good–bad distinction related to it has become increasingly hard to maintain. This also implicates the realities of sex work and the way sexual capital is being accumulated. One notable consequence of the ontological erosion of the boundary between gift and commercial logic that underlies sexual life has been the emergence of a market niche for a type of commercial sex that is more emotional and less mechanical. A good example of this multiplication of values in the sex trade is the market of legal brothels in the state of Nevada. Barbara G. Brents and Kathryn Hausbeck suggest that the managers of these brothels try to liken their sex businesses to any other service of the regular kind.[60] The dangerous, shabby, and unclean look of places where sex is being sold and bought is gone.[61] Instead, "[t]he setting encourages a more open, 'party' atmosphere and a more individualized, less rationalized interaction."[62] According to Brents and Hausbeck, Hof, one of the managers, even

> explicitly markets his brothel as a sexualized touristic destination, or, in his words, a "singles bar, except the odds are real good." . . . Hof argues that he is able to get more money from customers by approaching the "product" customers are buying as more of an experience rather than a sex act, maintaining that the customer "doesn't want to go to the room unless he feels close to you, or feels like you're friends, or there's some inner personal action going on there, okay?"[63]

Accordingly, not all sex workers experience trauma, direct exploitation, or complete lack of agency. In fact digital platforms for sharing amateur porn, such as OnlyFans, are based on an occupational model of self-employment and do not require face-to-face sex work. The performers (men and women alike) typically belong to the new middle class, which is drawn to flexible work schedules. Moreover, incomes earned are often invested in the workers' human capital, for instance education or training.[64]

This sense of choice and agency can be found in the more traditional forms of sex work, too.

As Teela Sanders suggests, through their emotional and sexual labor, some sex workers are able to resist being reduced to mere sexual objects.[65] Rather they act and think as service providers. By associating themselves with the "regular" service economy, some of them are able to capitalize on their own sexuality and increase their market appeal and financial gains. One Australian sex worker quoted earlier says: "I really like that I am very skilled and professional at what I do and that clients acknowledge this and are grateful for it . . . I am a sex educator and proud of it."[66]

In her path-breaking study on Silicon Valley sex workers, Elizabeth Bernstein has shown that these workers bring much more than the attractive appearance and sex organs to their sexual interaction with middle-class clients. They also bring emotional intelligence, people skills, and even cultural capital.[67] By extending the skills used in sex work and blending them, the sexual commercial exchange becomes more aligned with normative service work.

It would therefore seem reasonable to suggest that, for some sex workers, the typical "mode of coordination"[68] of sex work changes, as they manage to *accumulate sexual capital from their own sex work* without experiencing extreme social devaluation. Researchers have yet to provide a full sociological profile of those resilient sex workers. What *is* possible to determine, however, is that the scholarly debate about prostitution has recently been peppered with a new, neoliberal flavor. While the classic exploitation versus self-ownership debate is still going strong, new issues that pertain to identity and stigma management arise. This phenomenon could be seen as "a neoliberal take on prostitution" whereby the latter is discussed in terms of its singularity, of "how selling sexual favors affects the self-appreciation of the human capital engaged in such activity."[69] Clearly this is not relevant to the vast majority of those who are trafficked or have no other choice. Similarly, while many quarters of the sex industry, particularly the consumption of pornography and the use of sex toys, undergo social normalization, this does not mean that sex work has become a respectable line of work. But it is likely that, if bad sex is no longer that bad and if certain workers are not necessarily harmed or socially penalized for being involved in the sex trade, the sexual capital that is extracted from the sexual labor of sex workers could increasingly be seen as similar to the capital produced via regular interactive service work. This may be apparent in the phenomenon of soft prostitution, whereby middle-class young women and adult women in employment trade their sexuality for gifts or money.[70]

In fact sexual capital is created by sexed bodies and through the sexualized labor of workers in interactional service work.[71] Thus a fashion model interviewed for Kaplan's research on beauty and social class in Israel was reminded of her early days as a waitress. She very candidly admitted she was recruited for her extraordinary beauty and for the effect that her sex appeal had on customers, who, she fondly recollected, used to tip her very generously. Another telling example is the "staged seduction" taking place in women-only host clubs in Tokyo. As the ethnographer Akiko Takeyama contends, the male host was performing sexualized labor on her, hoping that she would become a regular at the club:

While I contemplated the hosts' intent, I noticed my knee was slightly touching Shin's. I straightened myself and slid my leg away. As I was drawn back into the conversation, my pant leg once again rubbed against Shin's. He inched slightly closer and leaned over to me. "Are you having a good time?" he murmured into my ear. I nodded. His whisper was ticklish, and, mildly affected by the alcohol, I became entranced by the sweet fragrance of his cologne. His subtle gestures had transformed the club's open space into an intimate environment where his proximity, whether accidental or not, seemed deliberate. Shin conveyed nothing substantive to me in his furtive whispers. However, by withholding the content of these exchanges from others, I grew attracted to him. These feelings arose because of—not despite—the existence of others in the open space. Shin created a fantasy, wherein my sensual experience and cognitive interpretation felt all-encompassing.[72]

Ashley Mears' ethnography of the elite global party circuit reveals a more familiar division of the same kind of sexualized labor. Mears shows that a global network of rich men—investment bankers, real estate moguls, and the like—is maintained to a high degree through the presence of "girls" on yachts in Saint-Tropez, at beach parties in the Hamptons on Long Island, or at fancy bars and restaurants in New York City. In this sexual economy, rich men use girls' bodies and looks to advance their social ties and business connections. Importantly, there seems to be a moral-cum-aesthetic hierarchy here: the more model-looking the girls are, the less directly sexualized or "stained" they are, and vice versa.[73] Tall, groomed, fashionable girls help break the ice between men, by adding to the surrounding a luxurious atmosphere. As Mears explains, "girls functioned as décor in two senses of the word: they were an embellishment that made the men look better than they were; they were also a mark of honor, a status signifier that caught the attention of other men."[74] Yet it is not just that beautiful girls are "making us look good, like furnishing the house," as one client in an upscale restaurant told Mears.[75] More than that, what looks high-status is pleasurable in itself. It simply feels good to be in the presence of beauty. In this regard, the women's bodies and faces are being extended and used to create the VIP atmosphere. Evidently, the more fake and cheap the girls look, the more they are believed to be paid. One of Mears' research participants described the perils of sexualized labor. Working as a cocktail waitress, her job was not only to serve the drinks but also to attract male clients to tables. These workers must constantly flirt with customers, and therefore have to be "a bit of little bit of a whore to handle it," she says.[76]

To summarize: we identify an emerging shift in the mode of coordination of sexual capital as a surplus value of the body, mostly in the increasingly blurring boundaries between sex work and so-called legitimate work in which the body functions as a sexual surface and presence is monetized as a sexualized presence. In some quarters of the sex industry, which is the main site for the production of this form of sexual capital, sex work becomes more akin to regular service work. This means that direct exploitation and work alienation are becoming less problematic for the sex workers involved. However, while they still produce monetary capital through the sexual acts their bodies perform, these workers are now faced with new problems, such as the growing demands for emotional labor, issues related to stigma management and self-branding, and so on. Importantly, these new problems are not dissimilar to those experienced by regular interactive service workers. Another way to describe this shift is to suggest that not only is sex work becoming more aligned with regular service work, but the reverse is also true: regular service work is also routinely sexualized, as we saw in the case of waitresses.[77]

Embodied sexual capital: Desirability, sexiness, and sexual know-how

The previous examples focused on sexual capital that is produced in the context of sex work or sexualized labor and is accumulated mostly by men who function like owners of human labor (although we have seen that in some contexts workers, too, are able to extract some of that value for themselves). The form of sexual capital discussed earlier in this chapter was coordinated under the assumption that sexual services and sexualized forms of labor are exchanged as part of monetized transactions. Now we focus on the third category, that of embodied sexual capital. Here the sexual encounter is not a transaction, something sold and bought, but part of a sexual relationship, even if fleeting. Sexual capital belongs to those who are more desirable than others, because they are able to attract more partners, or more desirable ones. This situation has been admirably well described by Michel Houellebecq in his novel *Whatever* (*Extension du domaine de la lutte*). As a reviewer put it in the *Independent*, Houellebecq's thesis was "that the sexual revolution of the Sixties created not communism but capitalism in the sexual market, that the unattractive underclass is exiled."[78] The French writer himself put it somewhat poignantly:

> We live today in a two-dimensional system: erotic attractiveness and money. All the rest, the happiness and the misery of people, is derived from this. . . . There are, as they say, sex supermarkets, who [*sic*] usually produce pretty elaborate catalogues of the porn supply; however, they lack the crucial thing. In fact, the consequence of the sexual quest is not the pleasure but, rather, the narcissistic reward, the prestige awarded by the desired partner for one's erotic superiority. This is the reason why AIDS didn't change a lot; the condom does reduce pleasure, but, unlike food products, the goal is not pleasure in itself: the goal is the narcissistic intoxication of the conquest. Not only that the porno consumer does not experience this intoxication, quite often he experiences the opposite feeling.[79]

The idea that sex is associated with, or involves, status competition was originally developed in the scholarship on mating, pairing, and marriage markets. A dominant perspective in this line of research draws on theories of social exchange and rational choice. This perspective suggests that actors aspire to maximize their utilities and strategically win status competitions, whether in upward mobility, as in the case of marrying "up," or merely to be considered a popular date, for example in systems of college dating and mating.[80] We, however, address a more recent iteration of the utilitarian approach, namely the sexual fields approach.

As we have already noted, the sexual fields approach investigates "the social organization of desire" within specific social networks of sexual interactions.[81] In this framework, a sexual field is a small-scale economy of social ranking with its own, internal rules of conduct, an economy organized around the desirability of self to others. Sexual fields could be urban localities, subcultures, nightclub scenes, or college dating systems.[82] In those arenas, some people are more sexually successful than others. They own more sexual capital. The emergence of sexual fields occurred in the background of the gradual autonomization of sexuality from religion. Inglis discusses the ways in which Irish sexuality gradually became differentiated from religion.[83] At whatever scale, the sexual domain is perceived as a quasi-autonomous social sphere, in which sexual capital is unequally distributed among actors.

James Farrer defines sexual capital as "a person's resources, competencies and endowments that provide status as sexual agents within a field."[84] Perhaps a testimony to actors' perception that sexuality is a field worth investing in and cultivating is the rise and flourishing of a formal "school" in seduction techniques, whose masters are known as pickup artists (PAUs). In 2018–19 the industry around this kind of coaching was estimated at $100 million dollars.[85] *The Game*, a book written by Neil Strauss in 2005 that offered techniques for success with women, is considered the catalyst of the current PAU wave. It sold 2.5 million copies.[86] These trends show clearly that sexual capital is something that actors are trying to seize.

If sexual capital is a resource that shapes who is more and who is less successful in this particular field, the "richest" is the one who accumulates most sexual capital on the basis of how attractive he or she is and how many partners he or she may have sex with. According to this theory, desirability itself enhances one's standing, furthers socio-sexual success within one's social circles, and is always relative to the desirability and success of others.[87] When sex is oriented toward status competition, actors in this area are perceived as agents who seek to maximize their sexual capital by approximating "the ideal physique; having the right clothes and accessories; and adopting the right postures, body language, vernacular, and speech patterns. Success breeds success: the more attention one receives in a sexual field, the more others are likely to perceive them as attractive."[88]

Indeed, most studies that take up a sexual fields approach foreground the embodied standards of sexiness in the specific sexual field. However, in her study of college hookup culture, Lisa Wade shows that sexual capital, the ability to attract partners on the hookup scene, was mostly related to players' having the right *affective* dispositions. Using the students' own stories, Wade shows that emotional aloofness and disengagement are the real currency of casual sex. Despite the significant long-term emotional damage of such arrangements, players on that scene still needed to perform their casualness and lack of care: "Being casual was not merely normative, but sexually charged. The more aloof students were, the more erotic status they could claim. And the alternative was not merely pathetic, but unsexy."[89]

The sexual fields approach has notable strengths. One is the emphasis on instances of social exchange, among participants of a specific field, of assets and competencies that grant differential sexual success. This is certainly a worthwhile attempt to take seriously the sociability of sex, to acknowledge on the one hand that sexual popularity carries the social advantage of making the person feel empowered and even more successful and, on the other, that the terms and conditions of desirability and popularity—whether of attractive bodies, of sexual know-hows, or of proper affective dispositions—are not universal. Rather these terms and conditions could be extremely conjectural. Another strength of this approach is the related contention that sexual capital is accumulated by the individual herself, as a personal, embodied attribute. Thus the sexual fields approach adds an important inter-individual and interactional layer to most social analyses of sex and sexuality, which usually opt for macro-structural explanations. This attempt to account for the shaping of collective sexual life through the everyday, at a mundane and local level, is commendable. By viewing sex as a personal social resource within a local ranking system, the sexual fields approach indeed advances our understanding of how everyday experiences of sexual desirability allocate and distribute social value. Yet, although this approach aligns itself with Bourdieu's sociology, it lacks a more developed and broader conception of power, of how other social forces, outside the particular sexual field under scrutiny, may shape hierarchies of sexual desirability.[90] Instead, players in a field are conceived of as too rational and utilitarian.

Crucially, embodied sexual capital is gendered, raced, and classed. Class is especially important, given the current dominance of selfie culture, both in the lives of young (and not so young) adults and in public and academic debates on young women's social media practices as forms of self-objectification. The debates and concerns around sexy selfies are a fertile ground for exposing what embodied sexual capital is, how it intersects with class, gender, and ethnicity, and how it is shaped in our cultural industries. If a society-wide process of cultural sexualization is underway, and if people from all walks of life both consume and produce sexualized imagery, this begs the question of who is considered sexy. Again, this is an important question to be raised, if we assume that embodied sexual capital is both shaped by social forces and shaping them.

In a project on the visual production of sexiness in culture, sexy selfies inspired by Instagram celebrity aesthetics were compared with photographs created by the researcher, herself a professional photographer. When asked in an interview what "sexy" meant to her, one participant mentioned "desirability and being 'seductive, but not trashy.'"[91] Here, clearly, the appreciation of sexiness is intertwined with class evaluation. Later in that article, researcher photographer Emma Phillips ponders on how she visually encoded similar middle-class perceptions into the professional photos she took of that (and other) participant(s):

I am conscious to encode these photographic collaborations with at least some of the signifiers which appeal to this aesthetic field—as an extension of my tastes and in the interests of my own cultural currency. I do this with lighting that evokes a sombre mood; lenses which create a sense of distance from, or unusual closeness to Simone; the addition of a mask on Simone's face or a trench coat worn provocatively; the moody cityscape; the intentional lensblur/movement; narrative suggestions and the privileging of a mirror . . . The [photos] are crafted with a conscious attention to a contemporary, professional portrait style with a chiaroscuro which promotes intrigue and evokes an emotional response. . . . I invite a deep looking. I want the viewer to question what is going on and to be seduced by the dark mood. . . . I have my audience in mind, and I know how to reach them. I am appealing to what Beverley Skeggs terms the "bourgeois gaze," though I am not conscious of this until I reflect upon it later. . . . I must consider if my own set of aesthetic codes helps to demarcate a class boundary which both affirms and extends my dominant cultural capital; and marginalises women's vulgar (I use the term here objectively) displays of sexuality. . . . It surely protects my place in the social field and reinforces class distinctions.[92]

As is the case with most middle-class judgments of taste, the research participants were also aware of the simultaneous "rightness" and power of such images to shape the aesthetic standards of sexiness. Women, and also men, must look and even feel a certain way ("seductive but not trashy," "fierce") if they are to be considered sexy by others and have sexual capital.

Embodied sexual capital can be aided by consuming various sexual lifestyle commodities and services.[93] Some of these commodities help consumers mold their bodies to appear sexier. A case in point is the rising popularity of female genital cosmetic surgery among middle-class women as part of a society-wide normalization of what Lindey McDougall calls "the clean-slit ideal." According to this ideal, which is promoted in the media (both mainstream and pornographic) and by medical doctors, an aesthetically pleasing vulva is hairless, smooth, clean, and minimalist looking. While vaginal plastic surgery is still a rarity, many women conform to this ideal by removing pubic hair, in an attempt to achieve the ideal of desirable femininity and increase their self-esteem.[94] Other commodities of sexual leisure promote the social ideal; accordingly, persons are valuable inasmuch as they are sexually competent and have developed the necessary "skills required to be a proficient sexual partner."[95] To be sure, sexual competence can be played out only in the private sphere of intimate relations, via both partners' embodied sexual performances. Sexual competence is a personal capacity. Because it is purely experiential, it usually has no semiotic visibility and for most ordinary sexual subjects (for whom sexual performances remain private) it cannot be read off their bodies. However, a large-scale industry of sexual self-help products has proliferated in popular culture to satisfy the requirement of "compulsory" sexual functioning and to teach us how to have a good sex life.[96]

In a world in which it is imperative to be sexually fulfilled, although this criterion is prevalent rather in long-term relationships, being "good in bed" becomes a valuable resource for women, too,[97] as the vast literature on casual sex reveals.[98] Thus, while the "enskilling of sex" can be placed in the first half of the twentieth century, it was first mediated through medical and psychological expertise, and it treated a woman's sexuality as "not just passive and latent, but integrally associated with her maternal and caring instincts."[99] But in the late 1960s this pedagogical role has moved to popular culture and less professional expertise.[100] As women's sexuality was affirmatively celebrated,[101] men and, increasingly, women were encouraged to take charge of their own pleasure and to work at it by using various commodities.[102]

We shall return to this type of personal, experiential sexual labor in the next section, where we discuss our fourth and final category of sexual capital. For now, it suffices to propose that sexual skills are commodities whose consumption is very much dependent upon class background and cultural tastes. In her ethnography of BDSM (bondage, domination, sadism, masochism) communities in San Francisco, Margot Weiss has shown that, as BDSM becomes a more institutionalized, mainstream and professional activity, it also comes to be described as a middle-class hobby: "practitioners work on their SM in self-conscious ways, mobilizing American discourses of self-improvement and education that dovetail with the emphasis on self-cultivation of Foucault's practice of the self."[103] Weiss goes on to show the panoply of BDSM practice classes, discussion groups, and member clubs that institutionalize the scene and remove its former kinky and abject associations. Thus, much as acquiring specific sexual skills enhances the field-specific sexual capital of BDSM practitioners, the BDSM lifestyle itself is based on these practitioners' existing cultural capital.

We argued before that sex produces capital either *directly*, as sex work, or *indirectly*, through the regulation of sexuality in the reproduction sphere so as to produce, collectively, docile wage workers who are willing and able to commodify their labor power. The same logic applies to the moment of consumption. Consumers nowadays purchase a whole panoply of sexual commodities and services. But sex is consumed not only via commodities used in sexual relations themselves. Some argue that, in the new economy, consumer culture at large creates a massive erotically charged fantasy work that structures collective consciousness and reproduces capitalism.[104] Paul Preciado has characterized this process as "high concentrations of sex-capital."[105] Preciado identifies a postindustrial "pharmacopornographic regime" that governs our sexual subjectivity and directs us to act in the interest of pharmaceutical and pornographic corporations. A good example, studied by several researchers, is the connection between the publishing of *Playboy* magazine (and other highly sexualized media products) and the rise of postwar consumer capitalism.[106] In other words, not only sex workers but also sex consumers co-create big capital. To give one single but telling example: in 2019 the global market size of sex toys was estimated at $26.6 billion dollars, a figure that is expected to grow in the coming years.[107]

Neoliberal sexual capital, self-appreciation, and employability

Thus far we have seen that sex is capital when it ensures marriageability or when it is extracted as *surplus value* from the sexual labor of sex workers (or from the sexualized labor of other service workers). We have also seen that, in some contexts, sex work shows some similarities with service and creative types of work. Like regular service occupations, sex work too requires emotional investment and self-branding skills in these contexts. Finally, we have also seen that, in *embodied sexual capital* sex, sexiness and desirability are procured mostly in the realm of consumption. Although interactional, this embodied form of sexual capital is not reproductive (when "animal desires" are used to ensure the docility of workers or the creation of future workers). Nor can it be reduced to a mere commodity, such as a sexual product or service, although it may definitely include those.[108] Rather, sexiness and sexual know-how are expressions of sexual tastes shared by like-minded people. Closely resembling cultural capital, this form of sexual capital is based on collective, classed schemes of valuation. It reflects the growing sexualization of culture, the fact that sex has become a significant part of the normal production of culture and of selves.

We now go a step further, suggesting that sexual capital is part of specifically neoliberal "desirables such as autonomy, esteem and capacities for self-expression."[109] These desirables are directly linked to employability. Employability is the bundle of personal achievements, skills, and attributes that may attract employers in a highly competitive employment market. Sociologists of labor have established that in the new economy the private sphere and the public sphere are endemically blurred. This means that workers are required to act as one-(wo)man brands. It is thus no longer just their labor power that employees sell, but their whole existential being, from which they are able to extract an economic value. When Lena Dunham uses her own tattooed naked body to play her alter ego Hanna, blurring the line between biography and art to create a TV series of worldwide success like *Girls*, she is in fact using her sexual self to produce a cultural commodity that caters to the habitus, at once sexual and professional, of the creative class.[110] More generally, it is increasingly necessary for individuals to build their independent brand and to constantly invest in their own employability.[111] Employees try to assume a better position vis-à-vis employers in the employment contract by acquiring not only the right look but also the right attitude.[112] We surmise here that a fully employable individual, capacitated to adapt to an unpredictable future, is one who is also fully sexual.

We have already seen that sexiness and good looks may come in handy for women not only in careers that involve display work for the beauty, sex, glamour, and fashion industries.[113] They are also increasingly significant in regular jobs, too.[114] But beyond the monetization of sexiness in the workplace, how can sexual experiences be useful for employment? It might seem absurd to suggest that the experiential dimension of sex may be capitalized for employment's sake. After all, sex is still a very private matter. Moreover, we are expected to act professionally at work at all times and, at a minimum, not to engage in sexual banter or harassment. So what is the connection between the private sphere of sexual experience and the public occupational sphere?

Indeed there may be a connection between sexuality and employability. To understand this claim we suggest only four possible directions. They are theoretical, but all four should be empirically investigated.

One connection could be that sex increases self-esteem, which increases self-confidence, which in turn projects competence. Dana Kaplan found that, to some extent, being sexually experienced or leading a less normative sexual lifestyle enables some individuals to feel self-assured and to accumulate this feeling for later use.[115] A second connection could be that sexuality expresses some kind of domination (especially in the form of the one-night stand, as Illouz has claimed in *The End of Love*). Thirdly, sex may be a way to exercise social competence, a much needed skill in the service economy. Given that sexual encounters demand a certain amount of mastery of social skills, and even seductiveness, these skills and seductiveness can be easily transferred to the sphere of labor.

Finally, good sex leads to greater job satisfaction. A group of researchers who studied the effect of (marital) sexual encounters on job satisfaction found that "employees experience a 5% increase in mood at work the next day for each time they engaged in sex the previous evening."[116] They go on to suggest that

> employees who seek advancement within their organizations or who rely upon their own work engagement to generate income (such as self-employed persons or those doing contract work) should be especially mindful of tending to their sex lives. Engaging in marital sex appears to create mood-driven positive outcomes the following day.[117]

If sex can create positive affects the next day, we may surmise that it helps generate income. It is thus reasonable to assume that sexual experiences add another layer to workers' employability.

In proposing the idea that sex contributes to employability, we return to a distinction we have drawn earlier but that got slightly blurred during our discussion of the various sexual capitals—namely the distinction between *sexiness* and *subjective sexual experiences*. As we have seen, sexiness as sexual capital (category 3) is the sexual power that some people may have in a given situation. The problem with sexiness as sexual capital is that it usually fades with time, especially for women.[118] This is because women's economic and sexual value is constructed mostly by men and for men. Moreover, there are still severe social and professional penalties for openly commodifying sexiness, even if this is voluntary.[119] Sexual *experiences*, on the other hand, are essentially internal to the self; they are long-lasting and are not specifically gendered. While sexual experiences are usually aroused in the company of others, the effects of these experiences and encounters are tied to our sexual subjectivity and can linger in our memory. Now, there is no denying that the distinction between objective realities and subjective experiences is purely analytic. Still, we maintain that "sexy" and "experiential" are two separate dimensions of sexual capital. As we make this distinction, we suggest that in neoliberal capitalism personal sexual experiences, and not just attractiveness, may enhance employability.

We suggest that in late modernity sex can be capitalized not just in sex work and sexualized labor, and not just as a consumer lifestyle choice (categories 2 and 3 respectively). Neoliberal sexual capital can be viewed as the sum of individually accumulated sex-related affective states that summon feelings of self-worth and self-determination, especially ones related to risk-taking, uniqueness, self-realization, creativity, and ambitiousness.[120] This bundle of sex-related affects is similar to what Pierre Dardot and Christian Laval term "the neoliberal 'performance/pleasure' apparatus," which compels neoliberal subjects to constantly have fun, to experiment, and to be creative.[121]

In the realm of sex, the neoliberal performance–pleasure apparatus has been addressed as a predominantly gender issue that pertains to the sexual agency of women.[122] The figure of the sexually agentic, empowered "alpha" (young) woman indeed attracts the public imagination. This public discourse directly associates sexual agency with professional success. Take for example this ad for Bumble, a dating app that encourages (heterosexual) women to "make the first move":

If you ask any random woman on the street, she will surely remember the first step she ever took. No, not her actual first baby steps! Rather, I am referring to that crippling moment when, in fourth grade, you stood there in front of your classmates to present your work. At first, you were so stressed out, that it felt as if your brain is about to melt. Still, you did it, and rocked it too. Or maybe at the office, when everyone else always got to do presentations, and you so desperately want to do that too, but convince yourself that you are just not cut for it. But you nevertheless approach your boss and he accedes, and you do it and you blow yourself away! It's just like that moment on a date when you are trying so hard to impress him, but wait till he kisses you first. Unless he kisses you, you won't feel like you succeeded. But there is this one time where you simply take the first step and kiss him. You say to yourself: hell ya!, this is what I want right now! Life is made of such small first steps. This is why we created Bumble. A social network in which women feel empowered to take first steps when it comes to love, work and life. So download Bumble and take your first step. Bumble, the first step is yours.[123]

To be sure, the chain of events portrayed in this piece of self-promotion leads from professional to sexual success (and not vice versa, which is what we suggest). However, both achievements are measured in terms of risk-taking and the agility one has for the game. Sex may thus boost self-confidence, but this has almost nothing to do with how the woman looks; more important is how daring she is. Thus the professional and the sexual spheres are almost blurred here and cannot be separated from each other. In this respect, Bumble treats sex as a playground for exercising those coveted neoliberal desirables of "autonomy, esteem and capacities for self-expression."[124] The Bumble ad is a product of its time. It echoes some joyful feminist calls to reclaim sexiness and to develop empowered sexual subjectivities. In this way of thinking, "sexiness is a way of being, a process, not a possession."[125]

Paradoxically, this feminist rerouting of "sexy" into the realm of what we call "sexual experience" fits perfectly with our understanding of neoliberal sexual capital. The fit is paradoxical because, precisely when critical feminist thinkers try to overcome the appearance-based "sexy" paradigm, this is also the moment when this existential way of "being sexy" becomes economically useful.

Bumble-style sexual empowerment notwithstanding, we contend that the ability to perform sexual autonomy, to be sexually creative and expressive, and, moreover, to capitalize on it is not specifically gendered. In fact class and class relations may be more relevant to this form of sexual capital than gender. Thus the effect of sexual experiences and interactions on current or future employment is already classed. Studies consistently find that sexual activities are divided by class.[126] This is precisely what we meant when we suggested earlier that sexual capital is a sort of embodied cultural capital (our category 3). However, we now suggest something more radical: only *some* subjects can gain economic returns on their sexual capacities and experiences.

Most able-bodied people do not encounter real barriers to engaging in sexual activities. Yet the reality is that not all sexual subjects can convert their experiences into entrepreneurial dispositions and employable skills. Mostly this path is reserved for those with a middle-class habitus. According to Beverley Skeggs, middle-class habitus enables displays of being "a good, interesting, adventurous, risk-taking person. Choosing danger, adventure and risk may enhance personal exchange-value and speed promotion for the middle class."[127] What is notable, then, is the significance of personal uniqueness to one's exchange value in the employment market.[128]

So far we have suggested that middle-class habitus builds on singularity and risk-taking. We have also maintained that sexual capital may enhance employability. But what exactly is the connection between middle-class habitus and sexual capital-related employability? Class relations are reproduced through everyday interactions—specifically those that take place at work. Traditionally, middle-class authority and social privilege have been established and reproduced within professional settings.[129] Yet the question is what constitutes middle-class authority now, as fewer middle-class subjects go through stable career paths and enjoy job security. When employment is so precarious, middle-class subjects are left with almost nothing but their own innate affective—and, in our case, sexually roused—capacities to restore their authority.

While there is an extensive literature on the neoliberal subject as a precarious self-entrepreneur destined to keep tending to her own employability, unfortunately there are hardly any empirical works that actually link sexuality and occupational entrepreneurialism in the direction we propose. It has indeed been argued that in current capitalism work has been eroticized as a form of personal freedom and inalienation. "Passionate" types of labor affect even sex work, as we have seen. Singularity is now a mode of production and self-identities have become means of production.[130] No longer exclusively perceived as the hidden kernel of a true self, sex and sexuality have now become objectified as lifestyle niche commodities, as improvable skills and techniques, as modes of personal communication, as paths to well-being, and as evidence of creativity, experience, and performable singularity. This comes close to Dowsett's contention:

> In creating a market for bodies-in-sex . . . in the production of selves through technology consumption, in performing sex online alone or with others, in marketing a self that is publically sexual, the increasing commodification of bodies and sex, beyond a simple notion of goods and services, illustrates that Braverman's notion was right about capitalist commodification and its unrelenting drive to draw more of life into its grip. But he was not at that time able to see in gesturing toward "culture, leisure and family life" the ongoing commodification of sex, sex acts and experiences, of sexually active bodies, the expanding market for sexual selves, and that one's

very sexual subjectivity would be increasingly shaped within the logic of market relations. Braverman was also not able to envisage a productive side to this process—productive of pleasure, adventure, sociability, innovation, social change, communication and connection. . . . It is the mutability of the self on these sites that is interesting: old certainties give way to creation and exploration, and this is disruptive of the sexuality and gender order—straight today, bi tomorrow; sadist today, sissy tomorrow. In choosing what we are, do and want sexually, we transform into a new product, marketed and available for purchase, and our pleasures expand in return. Commodification is the cost of our concupiscence, and sexuality continues to expand like the universe—our very own Big Bang theory of desire.[131]

In this lengthy passage Dowsett suggests that the idea that one's sex life represents one's inner, coherent, fixed, and unique core self has given way (even if not entirely) to a more performative understanding of sex and sexuality as a socially constructed yet fluid set of identifications. While we agree with Dowsett's assessment that some sexual identities may have become fluid and that the sexual sphere has become commodified to the point that personal sexual pleasures, identifications, and experiences participate in the branding of selves as open, free, and empowered, there is also a major point of difference between our approach and his. Dowsett does not clarify what he means by "we transform into a new product, marketed and available for purchase, and our pleasures expand in return." In that respect, his perception remains limited to the sexual field approach, in which "returns" have the form of more sexual encounters and greater social success *within that field*.

Moreover, as we have argued in Introduction, most sexuality scholars would be inclined to foreground the emancipatory or transgressive potentiality created by the emergence of radical sexual identities, somewhat more fluid and less binary. We, on the other hand, understand the extreme self-commodification of some of these identities as a form of neoliberal labor power and as a differential occupational advantage. For, as recent studies have shown, non-binary individuals, genderqueers, and other gender-diverse people endure many types of social discrimination in many organizational settings. Specifically in the labor market, growing evidence suggests that, while workplaces increasingly put "diversity" policies in place, on average transgender people are less likely to be employed, wage penalties for some sexual identities are still intact, and workplace environments are not always accommodating, as some people may be pressured to conform to binary gender norms.[132]

Unlike Dowsett, who understands sexual self-branding as something that remains limited to the inter-individual realm we discussed above, Rosemary Hennessy takes one step further, into a more structured realm of working life and organizational settings, also noted by Jacques Bidet.[133] She argues that non-normative sexual identities increasingly become an asset co-opted into the specifics of knowledge and creative economy production. Some workplaces even use workers' homosexuality as part of their "diversity" programs.[134] However, this is not exactly the same as arguing—as we do—that middle-class employability may now depend on affects associated with sexual self-appreciation.

One promising strand of research from which we can learn how neoliberal sexual capital is related to middle-class employability, and hence to the class structure more broadly, deals with college sex. Recent studies have shown that both men and women strategize their sexual couplings during their undergraduate studies (although women are more negatively affected by the hookup culture than men).[135] In their study on casual sex in an American university, Laura Hamilton and Elizabeth Armstrong found that, unlike students from lower-class backgrounds, upper-class students did not opt for long-term relationships.[136] The participation of upper-class women in the hookup culture allowed them to "have fun," be psychologically empowered, and, most importantly, dedicate more time to their studies and future careers instead of wasting their emotional energies on some man.

We have proposed that sex, which is coordinated and experienced in the private sphere, can be useful in the economic sphere as well, specifically in an unstable neoliberal labor market.[137] Such a view no longer considers the sexual sphere as auxiliary to the sphere of production, but as almost indistinguishable from it. This definition is at one and the same time economic, and thus similar to Bourdieu's, and non-economic, and thus different from Bourdieu's.[138] In the final analysis Bourdieu believed that all fields and their specific capital are secondary to the field of power. Economic capital is the basis of all subjective social classifications and life chances, and all non-economic capitals are translatable into it—and not necessarily vice versa.[139] But this form of capital assumes that there is no separate sexual field.

We might ask, what is the difference between our approach to sexual capital and the way Catherine Hakim connects sexual and erotic capital to the job market? To be fair, Hakim suggests that sexual capital includes "energy, erotic imagination, playfulness."[140] These components are quite similar to how we define neoliberal sexual capital. But her work is understood mostly to refer to the sexiness of women. Unlike in her approach, we assume that sexiness can be capitalized by men, too, and that sexual capital may be extracted from sexual experiences and interactions, and not just from "sexy" appearances. Finally, we believe that owners of sexual capital do not simply strategize in order to augment their capital or cash in on it in the job market. Employable sexual capital is not utilitarian. Rather, what motivates one to accrue it or to put it to use is not an interested behavior but habituation instilled by class dispositions.

5

Conclusion

Christianity privatized sexuality. But from that we have moved to an era where the sexual self is externalized, expressed in politics but mostly in consumer acts. With the triumph of Freudianism, the sexual self is no longer buried beneath one's public self.[1] It is no longer even an autobiographical project of finding one's truth, but has become a discontinuous series of performances, a "public proclamation of sexual identity."[2] While most critical sociological approaches to the social functioning of sex point *either* to socioeconomic injustices related on the one hand to sex and sexuality and on the other to the exchange of sex *or* to the marginalization and empowerment of sexual minorities, sexual capital is in fact advantageous only if we look at it as *both* a personal inner feeling *and* a psychic capacity that can be used as a source of authority when working life is dominated by short-term, project-based kinds of employment that lack a clear structure, an organizational setting, and continuity.

The theory of neoliberal sexual capital that we offer in this book thus proposes a radical political economy of sex.[3] It is radical because it challenges the prevalent view that sex is essentially a private matter, which has no bearing on how the social space is organized, particularly class relations at the macro level. In this respect, our approach differs from those advanced by human capital scholars. At first glance, in their focus on individual investments in various knowledges that enhance employment, human capital scholars seem to point in a direction similar to ours. They, too, look at hard-to-quantify employable skills that are privately held: credentials that, historically, have enlarged the bargaining power of middle-class employees in the heyday of Fordist class relations. Likewise, our theory links embodied attributes and employment. But, unlike human capital scholars, we do not assume the existence of a rational actor who consciously takes advantage of her or his sexiness or "performable identity."[4] Even if we take sexual capital to be individually accumulated, this view does not necessarily entail an economist choice theory approach to sexual capital. Unlike proponents of rational, utilitarian approaches to sexual behavior, we regard sex as something more than a matter of individualistic attempts to maximize one's capital, where atomistic actors calculate their investments while pursuing their interests.[5] We propose instead that sexual capital exemplifies more generally how middle-class workers, specifically those engaged in cultural and creative labor, use to their advantage, in a very competitive occupational market, various types of tacit knowledge and embodied capabilities—not necessarily ones that require formal training or prolonged periods of acquisition.

We assume that sex is capital not just when the sexual capacities and labor power of classed subjects are exploited by the dominant class—in other words we go beyond the view of sexual capital as surplus value of the body. Nor is sexual capital a purely personal asset, used and managed by rational autonomous subjects at an inter-individual level, through consumer culture, and in personal or occupational relationships, as some economists believe.[6] Rather, to the extent that aesthetic codes of sexiness and even of sexual know-how are gendered and classed, as we have shown in discussing our third and fourth categories, neoliberal sexual capital is part of the class structure precisely because it is accumulated by individuals in their everyday, intimate life. More than producing well-adjusted workers whose sexual desires are confined to the private sphere of intimate relationships and domestic consumption, neoliberal sexual capital is premised on the assumption that only certain subjects can use in the workplace, too, the sexual freedom they privately enjoy—and use it as human capital. By having sex, some people gain confidence and self-worth that make them more employable.[7]

Throughout this book we have repeatedly foregrounded the role of the sex industry in capital accumulation. But the sex industry explains only in part how sex is conducive to class structure. Yes, sex does sell, and the sex industry has greatly contributed to the subjugation of (mainly) poor women and an increasingly large pool of middle-class women. But in contemporary culture sex also epitomizes freedom, self-realization, empowerment, and creativity, the very same ideals of contemporary capitalism and, more significantly, the pillars of working life. By developing the concept of neoliberal sexual capital, we take seriously what feminists have argued for a long time: that the sphere of reproduction, or "life itself," is directly involved in sustaining the capitalist system and in creating capital. We can take this notion further and view subjective skills and practices as direct means of production within a "self-invented," "passionate," and creative working life.[8] Neoliberal sexual capital is but one example of a social reality in which particularly middle-class subjects, *both* men *and* women, must exploit their lifeworlds and identities in order to make themselves employed, especially in the creative professions. In this respect, sexual capital—an erotic attractiveness that involves either sexiness (usually for women) or sexual performance (usually for men) or both—has expanded; it is not only something exchanged between men and women in a way that reflects and reproduces gender hierarchies. Sexual capital also involves and implicates the totality of capitalist reproduction.

Notes

Notes to Chapter 1

1 This is what sociologists Alain Caillé and Frédéric Vandenberghe argue in the first part of their book *For a New Classic Sociology: A Proposition, Followed by a Debate*, New York 2021.

2 Paul Rutherford, *A World Made Sexy: Freud to Madonna*, Toronto 2007.

3 Ranji Devadason, "Metaphor, Social Capital and Sociological Imaginaries," *Sociological Review* 59:3 (2011), 633–54; Richard Swedberg, "Using Metaphors in Sociology: Pitfalls and Potentials," *American Sociologist* 51 (2020), 240–57.

4 Elizabeth Bernstein, "Sex Work for the Middle Classes," *Sexualities* 10:4 (2007), 473–88; Emily Chang, *Brotopia: Breaking Up the Boys' Club of Silicon Valley*, New York 2018; Yu Ding and Petula Sik Ying Ho, "Sex Work in China's Pearl River

Delta: Accumulating Sexual Capital as a Life-Advancement Strategy," *Sexualities* 16:1–2 (2013), 43–60; Amin Kalaaji et al., "Female Cosmetic Genital Surgery: Patient Characteristics, Motivation, and Satisfaction," *Aesthetic Surgery Journal* 39:12 (2019), 1455–66.

5 See Dagmar Herzog's review of historiographies of European sexualities, and specifically her summary of Callum Brown's book *The Death of Christian Britain* (2001), where Brown argues that around 1800 there occurred a "feminization of piety. Women became the arbiters and maintainers of religiosity on behalf of their families, and this role was accompanied by an emphasis on female sexual modesty and respectability. Female identity was thus grounded in the embrace of both religiosity and respectability" (Dagmar Herzog, "Sexuality in the Postwar West," *Journal of Modern History* 78:1 (2006), 144–71, here 152–3).

6 Catherine Hakim, *Erotic Capital: The Power of Attraction in the Boardroom and the Bedroom*, New York 2011, 6.

7 Catharine A. MacKinnon, "Feminism, Marxism, Method, and the State: Toward Feminist Jurisprudence," *Signs: Journal of Women in Culture and Society* 8:4 (1983), 635–58.

8 Pantéa Farvid, Virginia Braun, and Casey Rowney, "'No Girl Wants to Be Called a Slut!': Women, Heterosexual Casual Sex and the Sexual Double

Standard," *Journal of Gender Studies* 26:5 (2017), 544–60; Sabino Kornrich, Julie Brines, and Katrina Leupp, "Egalitarianism, Housework, and Sexual Frequency in Marriage," *American Sociological Review* 78:1 (2013), 26–50; Göran Therborn, *Between Sex and Power: Family in the World, 1900–2000*, New York 2004.

9 Surya Monro and Diane Richardson, "Citizenship, Gender and Sexuality," in H. A. van der Heijden (ed.), *Handbook of Political Citizenship and Social Movements*, Cheltenham 2014, 65–80; Diane Richardson, "Sexuality and Citizenship," *Sexualities* 21:8 (2018), 1256–60.

10 Monro and Richardson, "Citizenship, Gender and Sexuality," 68.

11 Ibid.

12 Richardson, "Sexuality and Citizenship."

13 Ibid.

14 Jyl Josephson, "Theoretical Perspectives on LGBTQ Movements," in William R. Thompson (ed.), *Oxford Research Encyclopedia of Politics*, Oxford, 2020, https://doi.org/10.1093/acrefore/9780190228637.013.1303; Monro and Richardson, "Citizenship, Gender and Sexuality," 68–71. For terminologies other than LGBTQ+ that speak to nonwestern local conditions and histories and are more in line with global South theories, see Surya Monro, "Sexual and Gender Diversities: Implications for LGBTQ Studies," *Journal of Homosexuality* 67:3 (2020),

315–24. For a European context, see Herzog, "Sexuality in the Postwar West."

15 We do so without denying the critical nuances that exist within queer theory more generally. See Jasbir Puar, "Rethinking Homonationalism," *International Journal of Middle East Studies* 45:2 (2013), 336–9; Leticia Sabsay, "The Subject of Performativity: Between the Force of Signifiers and the Desire for the Real," *The Undecidable Unconscious: A Journal of Deconstruction and Psychoanalysis* 5:1 (2018), 155–91; Carter Vance, "Unwilling Consumers: A Historical Materialist Conception of Compulsory Sexuality," *Studies in Social Justice* 12:1 (2018), 133–51.

16 Stephen Valocchi, "Capitalisms and Gay Identities: Towards a Capitalist Theory of Social Movements," *Social Problems* 64:2 (2017), 315–31, here 316. Importantly, "gay identity" serves us as an ideal type of host of other, emerging sexual (and gender) identities. Little by little BDSM, pan-sexuality, or asexuality—to name but a few of these emerging, fluid, and less defined forms of sexual identification—are solidifying into socially intelligible identities and categories. For a sharp analysis of how such inclusionary sexual–political projects are virtually self-defeating, see Sabsay, "The Subject of Performativity." For a political economy analysis of the embeddedness of asexuality in neoliberal capitalism, see Vance, "Unwilling Consumers." For the incorporation of queer fluidity into contemporary

commodity culture see Rosemary Hennessy, *Profit and Pleasure: Sexual Identities in Late Capitalism*, New York 2000, 68–9 (in ch. 4).

17 Since the 1990s, it is argued, claiming rights of sexual citizenship has tended to go in a reformist rather than transformative direction. Sexual rights reformists are usually "seeking inclusion into the mainstream," in order to remedy whatever inequalities may have been caused by cisgender and heteronormative policies (Josephson, "Theoretical Perspectives on LGBTQ Movements," 40).

18 Puar, "Rethinking Homonationalism," 337; Hennessy, *Profit and Pleasure*.

19 Richardson, "Sexuality and Citizenship"; Valocchi, "Capitalisms and Gay Identities"; Vance, "Unwilling Consumers." In the words of Rosemary Hennessy, "[s]ince exploitation is inherently an unequal social relationship (whereby some can only benefit at the expense of others), capitalism will always need some culturally oppressive ways to explain, justify, or legitimate this difference" (Hennessy, *Profit and Pleasure*, 90; see also p. 105 and cf. K. Duplan, "The Sexual Politics of Nation Branding in Creative Luxembourg," *ACME: An International Journal for Critical Geographies* 20:3 (2021), 272–93).

20 Lauren Mizock, Julie Riley, Nelly Yuen, T. Dawson Woodrum, Erica A. Sotilleo, and Alayne J. Ormerod, "Transphobia in the Workplace: A Qualitative

Study of Employment Stigma," *Stigma and Health* 3:3 (2018), 275–82.

21 Valocchi, "Capitalisms and Gay Identities," 316. Valocchi offers a nuanced postwar account of gay and lesbian changing regimes of inclusion and their relations to changing modes of capitalism. For a historical account of the origins of the modern gay identity and how it is associated with the rise of industrial capitalism in the United States, see John D'Emilio, *Sexual Politics, Sexual Communities: The Making of a Homosexual Minority in the United States, 1940–1970*, Chicago 1983. Rosemary Hennessy approaches this history from the perspective of consumerism and commodity culture. See Hennessy, *Profit and Pleasure*, 97–105.

22 Hennessy, *Profit and Pleasure*.

23 "Lifestylization" is a process that involves the collusion between the visibility of non-heterosexual identities on the one hand and, on the other, the promotion of specific consumerist practices and lifestyles associated with them. On the lifestylization of sexual politics, see D. Bell and J. Binnie, *The Sexual Citizen: Queer Politics and Beyond*, London 2000 and T. M. Milani, "Sexual Cityzenship: Discourses, Spaces and Bodies at Joburg Pride 2012," *Journal of Language and Politics* 14:3 (2015), 431–54. This process extends to other aspects of our everyday life as well.

24 According to this critical view, first set forth by Lisa

Duggan, "claims that particular nations or subjects are Modern increasingly rely on propositions of gender or sexual equality as either imminent or having already arrived" (Clare Hemmings, "Resisting Popular Feminisms: Gender, Sexuality and the Lure of the Modern," *Gender, Place & Culture* 25:7 (2018), 963–77, here 964; see also Lisa Duggan, *The Twilight of Equality? Neoliberalism, Cultural Politics and the Attack on Democracy*, Boston 2003; Tony H. Zhang and Robert Brym, "Tolerance of Homosexuality in 88 Countries: Education, Political Freedom, and Liberalism," *Sociological Forum* 34:2 (2019), 501–21).

25 Puar, "Rethinking Homonationalism." In this later piece, Jasbir Puar argues that her original concept has migrated and is now repackaged and sometimes misunderstood. Originally she wanted to explain how the notion of national liberal gay citizens "goes global, moreover, as it undergirds US imperial structures through an embrace of a sexually progressive multiculturalism justifying foreign intervention. For example, both the justifications and the admonishments provoked by the Abu Ghraib photos rely of Orientalist constructions of Muslim male sexuality as simultaneously excessively queer and dangerously premodern" (p. 336). For a critical review of the concept of homonationalism, see Josephson, "Theoretical Perspectives on LGBTQ Movements."

26 Gilly Hartal, "Gay Tourism to Tel-Aviv: Producing Urban Value?" *Urban Studies* 56:6 (2019), 1148–64.

Jasbir Puar has shown how queer tourism coming from the global North helps create "a queer cosmopolitan elite" and solidify a global gay identity. Gay and lesbian tourists, she goes on to claim, not only seek to realize their national sexual citizenship globally, but such manifestations of queer global mobility and visibility are underpinned by a vision of sexually modernizing global South others. See Jasbir Puar, "Circuits of Queer Mobility: Tourism, Travel and Globalization," *GLQ: A Journal of Lesbian and Gay Studies* 8:1–2 (2002), 101–38.

27 Nancy Fraser, "Crisis of Care? On the Social–Reproductive Contradictions of Contemporary Capitalism," in Tithi Bhattacharya (ed.), *Social Reproduction Theory: Remapping Class, Recentering Oppression*, London 2017, 21–36, here 33; Hemmings, "Resisting Popular Feminisms," 967–8.

28 Fraser, "Crisis of Care?" 33.

29 Vance, "Unwilling Consumers," 138–9; Sabsay, "The Subject of Performativity."

30 David Harvey, "The Body as an Accumulation Strategy," *Environment and Planning D: Society and Space* 16:4 (1998), 401–21.

31 In this we are influenced by Dagmar Herzog's contention that it is important to historicize (and, in our case, to sociologize) "not just sexual rights but also sexuality itself" (Herzog, "Sexuality in the Postwar West," 161).

32 Wendy Brown, "Neoliberalism's Frankenstein:

Authoritarian Freedom in Twenty-First Century 'Democracies,'" *Critical Times* 1:1 (2018), 60–79, here 62.

33 Eva Illouz, *The End of Love: A Sociology of Negative Relations*, Oxford 2019; Pierre Dardot and Christian Laval, *The New Way of the World: On Neo-Liberal Society*, London 2013; Martijn Konings, *The Emotional Logic of Capitalism: What Progressives Have Missed*, Stanford 2015.

34 Brown, "Neoliberalism's Frankenstein," 62. See also Paul Beatriz Preciado, *Testo Junkie: Sex, Drugs, and Biopolitics in the Pharmacopornographic Era*, New York 2013, 207.

35 Steven Seidman, *Romantic Longings: Love in America, 1830–1980*, New York 1991, 67.

36 Eva Illouz, *Consuming the Romantic Utopia: Love and the Cultural Contradictions of Capitalism*, Berkeley 1997; eadem, *The End of Love*; Hennessy, *Profit and Pleasure*.

37 Ken Plummer, "Sexual Markets, Commodification and Consumption," in George Ritzer (ed.), *The Blackwell Encyclopedia of Sociology*, vol. 9, Oxford 2007, 4250–2, here 4250–1.

38 See Dana Kaplan, "Porn Tourism and Urban Renewal: The Case of Eilat," *Porn Studies* 7:4 (2020), 459–73.

39 Feona Attwood, *Mainstreaming Sex: The Sexualization of Western Culture*, London 2009; Illouz, *The End of Love*; Preciado, *Testo Junkie*.

40 Andreas Reckwitz, "The Society of Singularities," in Doris Bachmann-Medick, Jens Kugele, and Ansgar Nünning (eds.), *Futures of the Study of Culture: Interdisciplinary Perspectives, Global Challenges*, Berlin 2020, 141–54, here 143.

41 Ibid., 145.

42 Stephen Maddison, "Beyond the Entrepreneurial Voyeur? Sex, Porn and Cultural Politics," *New Formations* 80–1 (2013), 102–18; Alyssa N. Zucker and Laina Y. Bay-Cheng, "Me First: The Relation between Neoliberal Beliefs and Sexual Attitudes," *Sexuality Research and Social Policy* 18:7–8 (2020), 1–7.

43 Dana Kaplan, "Sexual Liberation and the Creative Class in Israel," in Nancy Fisher, Steven Seidman, and Chet Meeks (eds.), *Introducing the New Sexuality Studies*, Oxford 2016, 363–70; Stephen Shukaitis and Joanna Figiel, "Knows No Weekend: The Psychological Contract of Cultural Work in Precarious Times," *Journal of Cultural Economy* 13:3 (2020), 290–302.

44 Michèle Lamont, "From 'Having' to 'Being': Self-Worth and the Current Crisis of American Society," *British Journal of Sociology* 70:3 (2019), 660–707.

45 Breanne Fahs and Sara I. McClelland, "When Sex and Power Collide: An Argument for Critical Sexuality Studies," *Journal of Sex Research* 53:4 (2016), 392–416.

46 Ibid., 408. In aspiring to understand how sex and power collide we also follow Viviana Zelizer's path breaking work on the interpenetration of market

and intimate social logics. As Zelizer explains, the realms of sex and economic transactions coexist regularly in a wide variety of interpersonal relationships. This is true to both sex work, and, most significantly, to more durable and broad intimate long-term romantic (and other) relations. This regular intersection explains why people constantly make what Zelizer dubs "good matches": we constantly work to make the economic and the intimate match each other in order to sustain our relationships. "Relations matter so much that people work hard to match them with appropriate forms of economic activity and clear markers of those relations' character" (p. 307). Making good matches is a constant, interactive everyday practice. It depends not only on our cultural understandings of appropriateness, according to the level or type of intimacy, but also on class, ethnic and other social positions (p. 307). Zelizer, V. A. (2006). Money, power, and sex. *Yale Journal of Law & Feminism*, 18(1), 303–315.

Notes to chapter 2

1 Faramerz Dabhoiwala, "Lust and Liberty," *Past & Present* 207:1 (2010), 89–179, here 156.

2 Ibid., 179; see also Stevi Jackson and Sue Scott, "Sexual Antinomies in Late Modernity," *Sexualities* 7:2 (2004), 233–48.

3 Adam Isaiah Green, "Introduction: Toward a

Sociology of Collective Sexual Life," in idem (ed.), *Sexual Fields: Toward a Sociology of Collective Sexual Life*, Chicago 2014, 1–24, here 7.

4 Illouz, *The End of Love*.

5 Pierre Bourdieu, *The Rules of Art: Genesis and Structure of the Literary Field*, Stanford 1996.

6 Max Weber, "Religious Rejections of the World and Their Directions" [1915], in Hans Gerth and C. Wright Mills (eds.), *Max Weber: Essays in Sociology*, New York 1958, 323–59, here 346.

7 Ibid., 347.

8 See Jeffrey Weeks, *Sexuality and Its Discontents*, London 1985, 12; Georg Simmel, "The Adventure," in Kurt H. Wolff (ed.), *Essays on Sociology, Philosophy and Aesthetics*, New York 1959, 243–58.

9 See Rosalind Ann Sydie, "Sex and the Sociological Fathers," *Canadian Review of Sociology/Revue canadienne de sociologie* 31:2 (1994), 117–38.

10 Most notably, albeit in very different ways, Anthony Giddens, *The Transformation of Intimacy: Sexuality, Love and Eroticism in Modern Societies*, Stanford 1992 and Michel Foucault, *The History of Sexuality*, vol. 1: *An Introduction*, London 1976. See also John Levi Martin and Matt George, "Theories of Sexual Stratification: Toward an Analytics of the Sexual Field and a Theory of Sexual Capital," *Sociological Theory* 24:2 (2006), 107–32, here 126.

11 Eva Illouz, *Why Love Hurts: A Sociological Explanation*, Cambridge 2012.

12 Werner Sombart, *Der Bourgeois: Zur Geistesgeschichte des modernen Wirtschaftslebens* (1913), as quoted in John Levi Martin, "Structuring the Sexual Revolution," *Theory and Society* 25:1 (1996), 105–51, here 115. Sombart's German original can be found at https://visuallibrary.net/ihd/content/pageview/3070 93?query=keusch.

13 Herbert Marcuse, *One-Dimensional Man: Studies in the Ideology of Advanced Industrial Society* [1964], New York 2013.

14 Andrew Sayer, "Moral Economy and Political Economy," *Studies in Political Economy* 61:1 (2000), 79–103, here 79.

15 Ben Fine, "From Bourdieu to Becker: Economics Confronts the Social Sciences," in Philipp Arestis and Malcolm C. Sawyer (eds.), *The Rise of the Market: Critical Essays on the Political Economy of Neo-Liberalism*, Cheltenham 2004, 76–106, here 77; compare Thomas Piketty, *The Economics of Inequality*, Cambridge, MA 2015.

16 Geoffrey M. Hodgson, "Conceptualizing Capitalism: A Summary," *Competition & Change* 20:1 (2016), 37–52; see Laurent Thévenot, "You Said 'Capital'? Extending the Notion of Capital, Interrogating Inequalities and Dominant Powers," *Annales: Histoire, Sciences Sociales*, 70:1 (2015), 65–76.

17 Thévenot, "You Said 'Capital'?"

18 Sayer, "Moral Economy and Political Economy," 94.

Notes to chapter 3

1 Valerie Traub, "Making Sexual Knowledge," *Early Modern Women* 5 (2010), 251–9, here 253.

2 Also Stevi Jackson and Sue Scott, *Theorizing Sexuality*, Maidenhead 2010, 139; Deborah L. Tolman, Christin P. Bowman, and Breanne Fahs, "Sexuality and Embodiment," in Deborah L. Tolman and Lisa M. Diamond (eds.), *APA Handbook of Sexuality and Psychology*, Washington, DC 2014, 759–804, here 760.

3 Janet Halley, *Split Decisions: How and Why to Take a Break from Feminism*, Princeton 2006. This definition is quite similar to Gayle Rubin's well-known "sex/gender system," understood as "a set of arrangements by which the biological raw material of human sex and procreation is shaped by human, social intervention and satisfied in a conventional manner" (Gayle Rubin, "The Traffic in Women: Notes on the 'Political Economy' of Sex," in Rayna R. Reiter (ed.), *Toward an Anthropology of Women*, New York 1975, 159–210, here 166).

4 David M. Halperin, "What Is Sex For?" *Critical Inquiry* 43:1 (2016), 1–31.

5 Halley, *Split Decisions*, 24; also Tamsin Wilton, "What Is Sex? Asking the Impossible Question," in eadem, *Sexual (Dis)Orientation*, London 2004, 54–75, here 56.

6 Rachel Wood, "Look Good, Feel Good: Sexiness and Sexual Pleasure in Neoliberalism," in Ana Sofia

Elias, Rosalind Gill, and Christina Scharff (eds.), *Aesthetic Labour: Rethinking Beauty Politics in Neoliberalism*, London 2017, 317–32.

7 Emily H. Ruppel, "Turning Bourdieu Back upon Sexual Field Theory," *Sexualities* 16 (2020), https://doi.org/10.1177%2F1363460720976958.

8 Lisa Duggan, "The New Homonormativity: The Sexual Politics of Neoliberalism," in Russ Castronovo, Dana D. Nelson, and Donald E. Pease (eds.), *Materializing Democracy: Toward a Revitalized Cultural Politics*, Durham 2002, 175–94; Claire Hemmings, "Affective Solidarity: Feminist Reflexivity and Political Transformation," *Feminist Theory* 13:2 (2012): 147–61, doi: 10.1177/1464700112442643; Jackson and Scott, "Sexual Antinomies in Late Modernity"; Eve Ng, "A 'Post-Gay' Era? Media Gaystreaming, Homonormativity, and the Politics of LGBT Integration," *Communication, Culture & Critique* 6:2 (2013), 258–83; Rob Cover, *Emergent Identities: New Sexualities, Genders and Relationships in a Digital Era*, Routledge 2018; Héctor Carrillo and Amanda Hoffman, "'Straight with a Pinch of Bi': The Construction of Heterosexuality as an Elastic Category among Adult US Men," *Sexualities* 21.1:2 (2018), 90–108.

9 Compare Gayle Rubin, "Thinking Sex: Notes for a Radical Theory of the Politics of Sexuality" [1984], in Carol S. Vance (ed.), *Pleasure and Danger: Exploring*

Female Sexuality, Boston 1984, 267–319 and Monique Mulholland, "When Porno Meets Hetero: SEXPO, Heteronormativity and the Pornification of the Mainstream," *Australian Feminist Studies* 26:67 (2011), 119–35. See also Feona Attwood and Clarissa Smith, "Leisure Sex: More Sex! Better Sex! Sex Is Fucking Brilliant! Sex, Sex, Sex, SEX," in Tony Blackshaw (ed.), *Routledge Handbook of Leisure Studies*, New York 2013, 325–36; Nancy L. Fischer, "Seeing 'Straight': Contemporary Critical Heterosexuality Studies and Sociology: An Introduction," *Sociological Quarterly* 54 (2013), 501–10; Jackson and Scott, "Sexual Antinomies in Late Modernity"; Steven Seidman, "Critique of Compulsory Heterosexuality," *Sexuality Research and Social Policy* 6:1 (2009), 18–28.

10 Karl Marx, *Capital*, vol. 1, Mineola 2019.

11 Rubin, "The Traffic in Women," 161.

12 Fine, "From Bourdieu to Becker," 79.

13 Hodgson, "Conceptualizing Capitalism," 43–4.

14 Ibid., 43.

15 Ibid., 44.

16 Thévenot, "You Said 'Capital'?" 66–9.

17 Pierre Bourdieu, "The Forms of Capital," in John G. Richardson (ed.), *Handbook of Theory and Research for the Sociology of Education*, New York 1986, 241–58.

18 See Eva Illouz, *Saving the Modern Soul: Therapy, Emotions, and the Culture of Self-Help*, Berkeley 2008; Michèle Lamont, *Money, Morals, and Manners: The*

Culture of the French and the American Upper-Middle Class, Chicago 1992.

19 Hodgson, "Conceptualizing Capitalism," 44; also Fine, "From Bourdieu to Becker," 79.

20 Anthony M. Endres, and David A. Harper, "Capital in the History of Economic Thought: Charting the Ontological Underworld," *Cambridge Journal of Economics* 44:5 (2020), 1069–91.

21 Thévenot, "You Said 'Capital'?"; Mike Savage, Alan Warde, and Fiona Devine, "Capitals, Assets, and Resources: Some Critical Issues," *British Journal of Sociology* 56:1 (2005), 31–47.

22 Thévenot, "You Said 'Capital'?" 70. By mode of coordination Thévenot means the ways in which disparate social activities, agents, and objects are ordered, put together, regulated, may become advantageous, etc. It consists of the concrete organizing principles, logics, and realms within which social actions take place. Markets are one such huge mode of coordination in societies; families too; and networks might be a third, more current mode of (social) coordination. In other words, a mode of coordination is a specific way of doing things as part of the general social order: specific ways of investment, of transmission and exchange, and of evaluating certain, field-specific practices. This is the main reason why, as far as Thévenot is concerned, there are various kinds of capital that cannot be reduced to economic and market-based capitals alone.

23 Scott Davies and Jessica Rizk, "The Three Generations of Cultural Capital Research: A Narrative Review," *Review of Educational Research* 88:3 (2018), 331–65; Gloria Kutscher, "Studying Diversity at Work from a Class Perspective: An Inductive and Supra-Categorical Approach," in Sine Nørholm Just, Annette Risberg, and Florence Villesèche (eds.), *The Routledge Companion to Organizational Diversity Research Methods*, New York 2020, 216–27.

24 Sam Friedman and Aaron Reeves, "From Aristocratic to Ordinary: Shifting Modes of Elite Distinction," *American Sociological Review* 85:2 (2020), 323–50.

25 Beverley Skeggs, "The Forces that Shape Us: The Entangled Vine of Gender, Race and Class," *Sociological Review* 67:1 (2019), 28–35.

26 Jon Beasley-Murray, "Value and Capital in Bourdieu and Marx," in Nicholas Brown and Imre Szeman (eds.), *Pierre Bourdieu: Fieldwork in Culture*, Lanham 2000, 100–19; Savage et al., "Capitals, Assets, and Resources."

27 See Rachel L. Cohen, "Types of Work and Labour," in Gregor Gall (ed.), *Handbook on the Politics of Labour, Work and Employment*, Cheltenham 2019, 261–80; Alan Sears, "Body Politics: The Social Reproduction of Sexualities," in Tithi Bhattacharya (ed.), *Social Reproduction Theory: Remapping Class, Recentering Oppression*, London 2017, 171–91.

Notes to chapter 4

1 Fraser, "Crisis of Care?"
2 Illouz, *The End of Love*.
3 See above; this point is also emphasized by Martin and George, "Theories of Sexual Stratification."
4 For a nuanced historical analysis of the social construction of sexuality before modernity, see Dabhoiwala, "Lust and Liberty"; Daniel Juan Gil, *Before Intimacy: Asocial Sexuality in Early Modern England*, Minneapolis 2006; and the essays in Satu Lidman et al. (eds.), *Framing Premodern Desires: Sexual Ideas, Attitudes, and Practices in Europe*, Amsterdam 2017.
5 Michel Feher, "Self-Appreciation; or, The Aspirations of Human Capital," *Public Culture* 21:1 (2009), 21–41.
6 Joanna Brewis and Stephen Linstead, *Sex, Work and Sex Work: Eroticizing Organization*, London 2000, 197.
7 Dabhoiwala, "Lust and Liberty."
8 See pp. 58–74 in this volume.
9 Feher, "Self-Appreciation," 23f. Viviana Zelizer called this the 'hostile worlds' belief, according "any mixing of intimate personal ties with economic transactions inevitably corrupts intimacy, and that invasion of commercial activities by intimate relations corrupts those activities as well" (Zelizer, p. 305).
10 Lauren Berlant and Michael Warner, "Sex in

Public," *Critical Inquiry* 24:2 (1998), 547–66, here 553; Gail Hawkes, *Sociology of Sex and Sexuality*, Buckingham 1996; Hennessy, *Profit and Pleasure*, 95; Thomas Laqueur, "Sex and Desire in the Industrial Revolution," in Patrick K. O'Brien and Roland Quinault (eds.), *The Industrial Revolution and British Society*, Cambridge 1993, 100–23.

11 Rubin, "Thinking Sex," 281–2.

12 Sheila Jeffreys, *The Industrial Vagina: The Political Economy of the Global Sex Trade*, London 2009.

13 Bernard Mandeville, *The Fable of the Bees; Or, Private Vices, Public Benefits* [1714], Glasgow 2019.

14 Dabhoiwala, "Lust and Liberty," 112–15.

15 Feher, "Self-Appreciation," 24.

16 See the chapters in Tithi Bhattacharya (ed.), *Social Reproduction Theory: Remapping Class, Recentering Oppression*, London 2017; see also Rhonda Gottlieb, "The Political Economy of Sexuality," *Review of Radical Political Economics* 16:1 (1984), 143–65; Kylie Jarrett, "The Relevance of 'Women's Work': Social Reproduction and Immaterial Labor in Digital Media," *Television & New Media* 15:1 (2014), 14–29.

17 Silvia Federici, *Caliban and the Witch: Women, the Body and Accumulation*, New York 2004.

18 Antonio Gramsci, "Americanism and Fordism," in idem, *Selections from the Prison Notebooks*, edited and translated by Quintin Hoare and Geoffrey Nowell Smith, New York 1971, 558–622.

19 Claudia von Werlhof, "Notes on the Relation between Sexuality and Economy," *Review (Fernand Braudel Center)* 4:1 (1980), 33–42, here 38. See also Dardot and Laval, *The New Way of the World*, 185–7; Sears, "Body Politics."

20 Jeffreys, *The Industrial Vagina*.

21 Rubin, "The Traffic in Women," 199.

22 Hakim, *Erotic Capital*; see also Roy F. Baumeister, Tania Reynolds, Bo Winegard, and Kathleen D. Vohs, "Competing for Love: Applying Sexual Economics Theory to Mating Contests," *Journal of Economic Psychology* 63 (2017), 230–41.

23 Green, "Introduction"; Adam Isaiah Green, "The Sexual Fields Framework," in idem (ed.), *Sexual Fields: Toward a Sociology of Collective Sexual Life*, Chicago 2014, 25–56; Valerie Hey, "The Contrasting Social Logics of Sociality and Survival: Cultures of Classed Be/Longing in Late Modernity," *Sociology* 39:5 (2005), 855–72; Ruppel, "Turning Bourdieu Back upon Sexual Field Theory." We discuss the sexual fields approach in the next few pages and will return to it later in the chapter.

24 Green, "Introduction," 28.

25 On the problem of scale in sexual fields studies, see Ruppel, "Turning Bourdieu Back upon Sexual Field Theory."

26 Tom Inglis, "Foucault, Bourdieu and the Field of Irish Sexuality," *Irish Journal of Sociology* 7:1 (1997), 5–28.

27 Willard Waller, "The Rating and Dating Complex," *American Sociological Review* 2:5 (1937), 727–34.

28 Green, "Introduction"; idem, "The Sexual Fields Framework"; Inglis, "Foucault, Bourdieu and the Field of Irish Sexuality."

29 Martin S. Weinberg and Colin J. Williams, "Sexual Field, Erotic Habitus, and Embodiment at a Transgender Bar," in Adam Isaiah Green (ed.), *Sexual Fields: Toward a Sociology of Collective Sexual Life*, Chicago 2014, 57–70.

30 Green, "The Sexual Fields Framework," 47.

31 Ashley Mears, *Very Important People: Status and Beauty in the Global Party Circuit*, Princeton 2020.

32 Plummer, "Sexual Markets, Commodification and Consumption."

33 Rachel O'Neill, *Seduction: Men, Masculinity and Mediated Intimacy*, Cambridge 2018.

34 Baumeister et al., "Competing for Love," 231.

35 Dana Kaplan, *Recreational Sexuality, Food, New Age Spirituality: A Cultural Sociology of Middle-Class Distinctions*, PhD Dissertation, Hebrew University of Jerusalem, 2015; eadem, "Sexual Liberation and the Creative Class in Israel."

36 See Baumeister et al., "Competing for Love."

37 Feher, "Self-Appreciation."

38 Kaplan, *Recreational Sexuality, Food, New Age Spirituality*; eadem, "Sexual Liberation and the Creative Class in Israel."

39 Ibid.

40 Feher, "Self-Appreciation"; Hey, "The Contrasting Social Logics of Sociality and Survival"; Kaplan, *Recreational Sexuality, Food, New Age Spirituality*.

41 Faramerz Dabhoiwala, *The Origins of Sex: A History of the First Sexual Revolution*, Oxford 2012, 181.

42 Ibid., 232.

43 But see Peter Gay, *The Bourgeois Experience: Victoria to Freud*, New York 1984, 133.

44 Hera Cook, *The Long Sexual Revolution: English Women, Sex, and Contraception, 1800–1975*, Oxford 2004.

45 Ibid., 65.

46 Sigmund Freud, "'Civilized' Sexual Morality and Modern Nervous Illness" [1908], in idem, *Sexuality and the Psychology of Love: With an Introduction by Philip Rieff*, New York 1963, 20–40; Martin, "Structuring the Sexual Revolution," 127.

47 Cook, *The Long Sexual Revolution*.

48 Freud, "'Civilized' Sexual Morality and Modern Nervous Illness."

49 Martin, "Structuring the Sexual Revolution," 115.

50 Gramsci, "Americanism and Fordism."

51 Lisa R. Pruitt, "Her Own Good Name: Two Centuries of Talk about Chastity," *Maryland Law Review* 63 (2004), 401–539, here 423.

52 Cohen, "Types of Work and Labour."

53 *The Report of the Commission on Obscenity and Pornography*, September 1970, 18–19, https://babel

.hathitrust.org/cgi/pt?id=mdp.39015036875279&vi
ew=1up&seq=37.

54 Joseph W. Slade, "Pornography in the Late
Nineties," *Wide Angle* 19:3 (1997), 1–12.

55 See Ross Benes, "Porn Could Have a Bigger
Economic Influence on the US than Netflix," June
20, 2018, https://finance.yahoo.com/news/porn-
could-bigger-economic-influence-121524565.html.

56 Visit https://www.pornhub.com/insights/2019-
year-in-review.

57 Harvey, "The Body as an Accumulation Strategy,"
406.

58 Jeffreys, *The Industrial Vagina*; Linda McDowell,
*Working Bodies: Interactive Service Employment and
Workplace Identities*, Oxford 2009. A good historical example is the separation of "reproductive
spaces from prostitutional spaces" in Puerto Rico
according to gendered, classed, and raced colonial
logic. See Preciado, *Testo Junkie*, 182–185.

59 Plummer, "Sexual Markets, Commodification and
Consumption."

60 Barbara G. Brents and Kathryn Hausbeck, "Marketing Sex: US Legal Brothels and Late Capitalist
Consumption," *Sexualities* 10:4 (2007), 425–39.

61 Dana Kaplan, "Recreational Sex Not-at-Home:
The Atmospheres of Sex Work in Tel Aviv," in
Brent Pilkey et al. (eds.), *Sexuality and Gender at
Home: Experience, Politics, Transgression*, London
and New York 2017, 216–231.

62 Brents and Hausbeck, "Marketing Sex," 433.
63 Ibid., 434.
64 Paul Ryan, *Male Sex Work in the Digital Age: Curated Lives*, New York 2019, 130.
65 Teela Sanders, "'It's Just Acting': Sex Workers' Strategies for Capitalizing on Sexuality," *Gender, Work, and Organization* 12:4 (2005): 319–42, here 322. Also, Zelizer pp. 308–310.
66 Brewis and Linstead, *Sex, Work and Sex Work*, 197, 233.
67 Bernstein, "Sex Work for the Middle Classes."
68 See Thévenot, "You Said 'Capital'?"
69 Feher, "Self-Appreciation," 30.
70 Kavita Ilona Nayar, "Sweetening the Deal: Dating for Compensation in the Digital Age," *Journal of Gender Studies* 26:3 (2017), 335–46; Franklin G. Mixon, "Sugar Daddy U: Human Capital Investment and the University-Based Supply of 'Romantic Arrangements,'" *Applied Economics* 51:9 (2019), 956–71. Zelizer, pp. 310–311.
71 Cohen, "Types of Work and Labour."
72 Akiko Takeyama, *Staged Seduction: Selling Dreams in a Tokyo Host Club*, Stanford 2016, xv.
73 This does not mean that there is no sexual violence in the fashion industry and that "real" fashion models do not encounter sexual abuse. In recent years this problem has surfaced. See S. Hennekam and D. Bennett, "Sexual Harassment in the Creative Industries: Tolerance, Culture and the

Need for Change," *Gender, Work & Organization* 24:4 (2017), 417–34.

74 Mears, *Very Important People*, 110.

75 Ibid., 112.

76 Ibid., 126.

77 Ibid.

78 "The Sex Export," *Independent*, Sunday, August 21, 2001.

79 Michel Houellebecq, *Interventions*, Paris 1998, n.p. For similar analyses of the functions of sexual competitions in the repertoire of Houellebecq, see Niall Sreenan, "Universal, Acid: Houellebecq's Clones and the Evolution of Humanity," *Modern & Contemporary France* 27:1 (2019), 77–93; Carole Sweeney, *Michel Houellebecq and the Literature of Despair*, London 2013; James Dutton, "Houellebecq, Pornographer? Monstration and the Remains of Sex," *Critique: Studies in Contemporary Fiction* (2020), 1–13. doi:10.1080/00111619.2020.1858748.

80 Waller, "The Rating and Dating Complex."

81 Martin and George, "Theories of Sexual Stratification," 108; Adam Isaiah Green, "Erotic Habitus: Toward a Sociology of Desire," *Theoretical Sociology* 37 (2008), 597–626; idem, "The Sexual Fields Framework."

82 Ruppel, "Turning Bourdieu Back upon Sexual Field Theory."

83 Inglis, "Foucault, Bourdieu and the Field of Irish Sexuality."

84 James Farrer, "A Foreign Adventurer's Paradise? Interracial Sexuality and Alien Sexual Capital in Reform Era Shanghai," *Sexualities* 13:1 (2010), 69–95, here 75.

85 See Sirin Kale, "50 Years of Pickup Artists: Why Is the Toxic Skill Still so in Demand," *Guardian*, November 5, 2019, https://www.theguardian.com /lifeandstyle/2019/nov/05/pickup-artists-teaching -men-approach-women-industry-street-harass ment.

86 Zing Tsjeng, "Men Are Still Spending Obscene Amounts of Money to Become Pick-Up Artists," June 15, 2018, https://www.vice.com/en/article /gyk37y/pickup-artist-study-rachel-oneill-seduc tion-book; Neil Strauss, *The Game: Penetrating the Secret Society of Pickup Artists*, New York 2005.

87 Green, "Introduction," 39.

88 Lisa Wade, "Doing Casual Sex: A Sexual Fields Approach to the Emotional Force of Hookup Culture," *Social Problems* 68:1 (2021), 185–201, here 187.

89 Ibid.

90 Ruppel, "Turning Bourdieu Back upon Sexual Field Theory."

91 Emma Phillips, "'It's Classy Because You Can't See Things': Data from a Project Co-Creating Sexy Images of Young Women," *Feminist Media Studies* 2020, 1–16, here 8, doi: 10.1080/14680777.2020.18 38597.

92 Ibid., 9. On the "bourgeois gaze," see Beverley Skeggs, "Imagining Personhood Differently: Person Value and Autonomist Working-Class Value Practices," *Sociological Review* 59:3 (2011), 496–513, here 496.

93 Illouz, *Saving the Modern Soul*; eadem, *The End of Love*; William Mazzarella, "Citizens Have Sex, Consumers Make Love: Marketing KamaSutra Condoms in Bombay," in Brian Moeran (ed.), *Asian Media Productions*, Richmond 2001, 168–96.

94 Lindy McDougall, *The Perfect Vagina: Cosmetic Surgery in the Twenty-First Century*, Bloomsbury 2021.

95 Ruth Lewis, Cicely Marston, and Kaye Wellings, "Bases, Stages and 'Working Your Way Up': Young People's Talk about Non-Coital Practices and 'Normal' Sexual Trajectories," *Sociological Research Online* 18:1 (2013), para 5.2.

96 Rosalind Gill, "Mediated Intimacy and Postfeminism: A Discourse Analytic Examination of Sex and Relationships Advice in a Women's Magazine," *Discourse and Communication* 3:4 (2009), 345–69; Elizabeth Goren, "America's Love Affair with Technology: The Transformation of Sexuality and the Self over the 20th Century," *Psychoanalytic Psychology* 20:3 (2003), 487–508.

97 Gill, "Mediated Intimacy and Postfeminism."

98 See Elizabeth A. Armstrong, Paula England, and Alison C. K. Fogarty, "Accounting for Women's

Orgasm and Sexual Enjoyment in College Hookups and Relationships," *American Sociological Review* 77:3 (2012), 435–62.

99 Hawkes, *Sociology of Sex and Sexuality*, 95.

100 Illouz, *Saving the Modern Soul*.

101 Jennifer Scanlon, "Sexy from the Start: Anticipatory Elements of Second Wave Feminism," *Women's Studies* 38:2 (2009), 127–50.

102 Gill, "Mediated Intimacy and Postfeminism"; Rosalind Gill and Christina Scharff (eds.), *New Femininities: Postfeminism, Neoliberalism, and Subjectivity*, London 2011; Melissa Tyler, "Managing between the Sheets: Lifestyle Magazines and the Management of Sexuality in Everyday Life," *Sexualities* 7:1 (2004), 81–106.

103 Margot Weiss, *Techniques of Pleasure: BDSM and the Circuits of Sexuality*, Durham 2011, 76.

104 Adam Arvidsson, "Netporn: The Work of Fantasy in the Information Society," in K. Jacobs, M. Janssen, and M. Pasquinelli (eds.), *C'LICK ME: A Netporn Studies Reader*, Amsterdam 2007, 69–76: 70; Hennessy, *Profit and Pleasure*, 94–110.

105 Preciado, *Testo Junkie*, 33.

106 Gail Dines, "'I Buy It for the Articles': Playboy Magazine and the Sexualization of Consumerism," in Gail Dines and Jean M. Humes (eds.), *Gender, Race, and Class in Media: A Critical Reader*, Thousand Oaks 1995, 254–62; Preciado, *Testo*

Junkie; Kaplan, *Recreational Sexuality, Food, New Age Spirituality*.

107 See "Sex Toys Market Size, Share & Trends Analysis Report," https://www.grandviewresearch.com/industry-analysis/sex-toys-market.

108 To follow the example we have provided in the last section, BDSM practitioners may consume sexual commodities such as special gear, training workshops, etc.

109 Rosemary Crompton, "Class and Employment," *Work, Employment and Society* 24:1 (2010), 9–26, here 21.

110 Maria San Filippo, *Provocateurs and Provocations: Screening Sex in 21st Century Media*, Bloomington 2021, 171–2; Christopher Lloyd, "Sexual Perversity in New York?" in M. Nash and I. Whelehan (eds), *Reading Lena Dunham's Girls*, Cham 2017, 197–207, https://doi.org/10.1007/978-3-319-52971-4_14; Rosalind Gill, "Afterword: Girls: Notes on Authenticity, Ambivalence and Imperfection," in M. Nash and I. Whelehan (eds), *Reading Lena Dunham's Girls*, Cham 2017, 225–42.

111 Jane Artess, Tristram Hooley, and Robin Mellors-Bourne, "Employability: A Review of the Literature 2012 to 2016—A Report for the Higher Education Academy," ERIC 2017, https://eric.ed.gov/?id=ED574372; Ilana Gershon, *Down and Out in the New Economy: How People Find (or Don't Find) Work Today*, Chicago 2017.

112 Peter Bloom, "Fight for Your Alienation: The Fantasy of Employability and the Ironic Struggle for Self-Exploitation," *Ephemera: Theory & Politics in Organizations* 13:4 (2013), 785–807, here 796.

113 Ashley Mears, *Pricing Beauty: The Making of a Fashion Model*, Berkeley 2011; eadem, *Very Important People*.

114 Scott Freng and David Webber, "Turning Up the Heat on Online Teaching Evaluations: Does 'Hotness' Matter?" *Teaching of Psychology* 36:3 (2009), 189–93; Catherine Hakim, "Erotic Capital," *European Sociological Review* 26:5 (2010), 499–518; eadem, "Erotic Capital, Sexual Pleasure, and Sexual Markets," in Osmo Kontula (ed.), *Pleasure and Health: Nordic Association for Clinical Sexology* (Conference Proceedings), Helsinki 2012, 27–44, http://nacs.eu/data/nacs_final_sec_edit_web.pdf; Chris Warhurst and Dennis Nickson, "'Who's Got the Look?' Emotional, Aesthetic and Sexualized Labour in Interactive Services," *Gender, Work and Organization* 16:3 (2009), 385–404.

115 Kaplan, *Recreational Sexuality, Food, New Age Spirituality*; eadem, "Sexual Liberation and the Creative Class in Israel."

116 Keith Leavitt, Christopher Barnes, Trevor Watkins, and David Wagner, "From the Bedroom to the Office: Workplace Spillover Effects of Sexual Activity at Home," *Journal of Management* 45:3 (2019), 1173–92, here 1185.

117 Ibid., 1186.

118 Illouz, *The End of Love*.

119 A story in the *New York Times* reported that, during the 2020 economic crisis caused by the COVID-19 pandemic, women who lost their jobs turned to OnlyFans. One of the interviewees "worries that her presence on the platform will make it more difficult for her to be hired for traditional jobs in the future. 'If you're looking for a 9 to 5, they might not hire you if they find out you have an OnlyFans,' she said. 'They may not want you if they know you're a sex worker'" (https://www.nytimes.com/2021/01/13/business/onlyfans-pandemic-users.html).

120 Kaplan, *Recreational Sexuality, Food, New Age Spirituality*; eadem, "Sexual Liberation and the Creative Class in Israel."

121 Dardot and Laval, *The New Way of the World*, 312.

122 Zucker and Bay-Cheng, "Me First."

123 See https://www.haaretz.co.il/digital/podcast/PODCAST-1.9388997.

124 Crompton, "Class and Employment," 21.

125 Sheila Lintott and Sherri Irvin, "Sex Object and Sexy Subjects: A Feminist Reclamation of Sexiness," in Sherri Irvin (ed.), *Body Aesthetics*, Oxford 2016, 299–318, here 310.

126 Chang, *Brotopia*; Alfred C. Kinsey, Wardell B. Pomeroy, and Clyde E. Martin, *Sexual Behavior in*

the Human Male, Philadelphia 1948; Elisabeth Sheff and Corie Hammers, "The Privilege of Perversities: Race, Class and Education among Polyamorists and Kinksters," *Psychology and Sexuality* 2:3 (2011), 198–223.

127 Beverley Skeggs, "The Making of Class and Gender through Visualizing Moral Subject Formation," *Sociology* 39:5 (2005), 965–82, here 971.

128 See also Hey, "The Contrasting Social Logics of Sociality and Survival."

129 Jacques Bidet, *Foucault with Marx*, London 2016, 138.

130 Lisa Adkins and Celia Lury, "The Labour of Identity: Performing Identities, Performing Economies," *Economy and Society* 28:4 (1999), 598–614; Lisa Adkins, "Sexuality and Economy: Historicisation vs. Deconstruction," *Australian Feminist Studies* 17:37 (2002), 31–41; Hennessy, *Profit and Pleasure*; Hemmings, "Affective Solidarity."

131 Gary W. Dowsett, "The Price of Pulchritude, the Cost of Concupiscence: How to Have Sex in Late Modernity," *Culture, Health and Sexuality* 17:S1 (2014), 5–19, here 12.

132 See Catherine J. Abe and Louise Oldridge, "Non-Binary Gender Identities in Legislation, Employment Practices and HRM Research," in Stefanos Nachmias and Valery Caven (eds.), *Inequality and Organizational Practice*, Cham, 2019, 89–114; Robin C. Ladwig, "Proposing the Safe

and Brave Space for Organisational Environment: Including Trans* and Gender-Diverse Employees in Institutional Gender Diversification," *Gender in Management: An International Journal* (2021), doi: 10.1108/GM-06-2020-0199; Danielle C. Lefebvre and José F. Domene, "Workplace Experiences of Transgender Individuals: A Scoping Review," *Asia Pacific Career Development Journal* 3:1 (2020), 2–30; M. I. Suárez, G. Marquez-Velarde, C. Glass, and G. H. Miller, "Cis-Normativity at Work: Exploring Discrimination against US Trans Workers," *Gender in Management: An International Journal* (2020), https://doi.org/10.1108/GM-06-2020-0201; Sean Waite, John Ecker, and Lori E. Ross, "A Systematic Review and Thematic Synthesis of Canada's LGBTQ2S+ Employment, Labour Market and Earnings Literature," *PloS One* 14:10 (2019), e0223372.

133 Hennessy, *Profit and Pleasure*; Bidet, *Foucault with Marx*.

134 Adkins, "Sexuality and Economy."

135 See Wade, "Doing Casual Sex."

136 Laura Hamilton and Elizabeth A. Armstrong, "Gendered Sexuality in Young Adulthood: Double Binds and Flawed Options," *Gender and Society* 23:5 (2009), 589–616.

137 Kaplan, *Recreational Sexuality, Food, New Age Spirituality*; Markella B. Rutherford, "The Social Value of Self-Esteem," *Society* 48:5 (2011), 407–12.

138 Our theory is indebted to Bourdieu's theory of field-specific capitals but at the same time departs from it. For Bourdieu, field-specific forms of capital are hard to acquire when competences to be a strong player in these fields are monopolized by a few. Such accumulated capitals might eventually yield general social benefits. However, we believe that adopting a Bourdieusian approach to sexual capital is better suited for explaining processes of domination, legitimation, and the naturalization of systemic inequalities. While for Bourdieu economic capital is key, his work details how non-economic capitals, too, delineate symbolic boundaries between social classes and in this way reproduce the symbolic and the real power of the dominant class. In other words, Bourdieu's is a theory of class domination. Bourdieu's broader project has been to carefully detail the mechanisms through which non-economic advantages (capital) reproduce the class structure. This approach is premised on the assumption that culture at large and the economy, or the spheres of reproduction and production, are separated (see Kaplan, *Recreational Sexuality, Food, New Age Spirituality*). But, as we stated throughout this book, in late modernity this presupposition is hard to maintain even from a critical point of view. This also changes the meaning of sexual capital.

139 See also Floya Anthias, "Hierarchies of Social Location, Class and Intersectionality: Towards a

Translocational Frame," *International Sociology* 28:1 (2013), 121–38, here 122.

140 Hakim, *Erotic Capital*, 22.

Notes to Chapter 5

1 Illouz, *Saving the Modern Soul*.

2 Goren, "America's Love Affair with Technology," 497.

3 Sayer, "Moral Economy and Political Economy."

4 Adkins, "Sexuality and Economy," 38.

5 See Baumeister et al., "Competing for Love"; Edward O. Laumann, John Gagnon, Robert Michael, and Stuart Michaels, *The Social Organization of Sexuality: Sexual Practices in the United States*, Chicago 1994, 8–15.

6 Baumeister at al., "Competing for Love"; Gary Becker, *Accounting for Tastes*, Cambridge, MA 1996, 4–5, 7; Hakim, *Erotic Capital*; Outi Sarpila, "Attitudes towards Performing and Developing Erotic Capital in Consumer Culture," *European Sociological Review* 30:3 (2013), 302–14.

7 Kaplan, *Recreational Sexuality, Food, New Age Spirituality*.

8 Angela McRobbie, *Be Creative: Making a Living in the New Culture Industries*, Cambridge, MA 2016, 61.